THE MODERN CHINESE FAMILY

BY: WAI-KIN CHE

PALO ALTO, CALIFORNIA
1979

PUBLISHED BY

R & E RESEARCH ASSOCIATES, INC.
936 INDUSTRIAL AVENUE
PALO ALTO, CALIFORNIA 94303

PUBLISHERS

ROBERT D. REED AND ADAM S. ETEROVICH

Library of Congress Card Catalog Number
77-91415

I.S.B.N.
0-88247-554-1

Copyright 1979
By
Wai-Kin Che

DEDICATION

For my sister Vicki K.W. Che

PREFACE

Anyone who wants to understand the life and society of the Chinese should first study the Chinese family. The Chinese society is "familistic" in that other social structures ramify from the family. Throughout his whole life, a person is surrounded by the influence of his family. There is a common belief that the persistence of China and its brilliant culture for the past two thousand years is the merit of the family institution. The significant contribution of the Chinese family has stabilized and perpetuated the Chinese society. However, very few researches have been conducted on the Chinese family.

By the turn of this century, the Chinese family had undergone many changes, due to such influences as Western culture, industrialization and urbanization. More drastic changes occurred after the Chinese Communists took over the China Mainland in 1949. The Chinese Communists have carried out their plans to change the family based on the Communist model. In 1950 a new Marriage Law was promulgated. In the 1960's and 1970's, the age and sex hierarchies, the most basic support of the Chinese family, were under attack. In Taiwan, the Chinese family has undergone spontaneous changes under the influence of Western culture, industrialization and urbanization. As a result, the age and sex hierarchies in the family have been weakened in the educated class living in the city.

In this book, the changes in the age and sex hierarchies in the 1960's and 1970's are examined. Also the relationship between education and the family is explored. There has been a strong affinity between education and the family in China as the former has been supported by the latter. Education was the proper way leading to the civil service in traditional China which was highly rewarded and valued. Besides, education has been a useful channel for social mobility, socio-economic betterments and an important agency for socialization.

In most societies there exist the ideal as well as the real cultures. The ideal culture includes formally approved values and norms that people are supposed to follow; the real culture consists of those they actually practice. One common source of strain in a society is the discrepancy between these two cultures. In traditional China, the national (central) government assumed the duty to establish the ideal family structure and the educational thought of the nation for the purpose of controlling the country. Such a practice was also perpetuated in Republican and Communist China. When the Chinese Communists planned to generate changes in the family and education in the China Mainland, they greatly publicized the ideal structure of the family and educational thought. In this book, the discrepancies between the ideal and the actual structures will be examined.

The author would like to express his sincere appreciation to those people who gave assistance in this research. The staff members of the Universities Service Center, Hong Kong, offered many services, but especially helpful by supplying data on the family and education of Communist China. Several faculty members of the Sociology Department of National Taiwan University likewise provided considerable material for the study on the family in Taiwan. Dr. Roderic C. Duchemin gave generous and important advice besides editing the manuscript. Dr. Robert H. Detrick made constructive comments and suggestions, and Mr. Andrew Yeung spent valuable time in proofreading the manuscript.

In credit for the positive features of the book, all of the above rightly share. For any errors or weaknesses, the author alone accepts responsibility.

TABLE OF CONTENTS

CHAPTER 1

INTRODUCTION TO THE STUDY

The traditional Chinese family has been well known for its close and intimate relationships, filial piety and loyalty, and the dominance of the male and senior members (2, 16, 17, 41). These characteristics extended to the larger kin and clan circles. These ties had direct and indirect influences upon the individual throughout his life. The family was a unit of economic production in the agrarian society and to a very large extent performed the function of socialization of its members. The values and norms for socialization were the teachings and ethics of Confucius. The traditional Chinese families were also semi-autonomous units in the traditional society (8, pp. 19-24; 41, p. 20).

By the turn of the century, long before the Chinese Communists took over the China Mainland in 1949, the Chinese family had been changing spontaneously. The forces for the changes were mainly the influence of western culture when the Chinese intellectuals first contacted western ideas and industrialization and urbanization (41, pp. 10-11). Even today the Chinese family in Taiwan continues to change as a result of these factors. Western ideals and values have had considerable influence on the younger generations.

A transition of the Chinese family has occurred since 1949 when the Chinese Communists took over the China Mainland. The Chinese Communists have planned to reshape the family and have used propanganda, mass movements, political, legal, and social pressure and forces to make change in the family (41, p. 19). The purpose of the Communist policy in reshaping the traditional family has been to prepare for the construction of an industrial society which would not be retarded by strong kinship ties. The Communists want no competition for loyalty and allegiance to the state and the Communist Party (41, p. 19). Also, they want to establish the Communist model of the family which would put the state and Communism in the first place. The establishment of the people's communes in 1959 and the nationalization of industries and commerce have had important impact on the Chinese family. Changes in the Chinese family have been influenced by education to a large extent. The Communists have made use of the school, from nursery to the university, to indoctrinate the children and the young people with the ideology of Communism (41, pp. 109-171).

Education and the family have been closely related in China and the relationships have continued even in the 1960's and 1970's. The Confucian school of educational thought has dominated the education in traditional, Republican and Nationalist China and has been supported by the rulers and the upper and middle classes. The opportunity to receive higher and professional education has become the privileges of the upper and upper middle classes (15). In Communist China, the Chinese Communists tried to reverse such a tradition and have permitted only the working classes to receive professional and higher education (7, pp.

1

19-21).

Over the past twenty-five years, the family revolution in Communist China could roughly be divided into three periods. Between 1950 and 1958 there was the period of the Marriage Law Movement. During this period the state made every effort to change the traditional marriage and family institutions by means of legislative and political pressure and mass persuasion and propaganda. The second period was that of the Great Leap Forward, and the establishment of the communes in 1958. A "new" type of socialist or communistic family was established as a model. The third period began with the Cultural Revolution in 1966. The aim for the changes was to destroy the sex hierarchy and to establish equality between the sexes in the family. In 1966 the attack on the age hierarchy-the other basic support of the traditional family-also began (40, p. 3).

For a generation in the sociological literature China has provided the example of a "familistic" society, one in which the family, and the kinship system ramifying from it, had an unusually strategic position in the total society (41, p. v). Since the family has been a very important and basic institution in China, it has undergone many changes by the turn of the century, especially in Communist China since 1949 and in the 1960's and 1970's. It is essential to examine those changes because they will directly and indirectly influence the social structure and destiny of the nation.

Purpose of the Study

The purpose of this study was to examine some of the important changes in the family in Nationalist China and Communist China, with special emphases on the period from 1959 to 1975.

There were five sub-purposes of the study:

(1) to present an overview of the traditional family as a common background for the comparison of the changes in the family in Nationalist China and Communist China;

(2) to identify the changes of the ideal family structures in the age and sex hierarchies;

(3) to identify the discrepancies between the ideal and the actual family structure in the age and sex hierarchies;

(4) to identify the relationship and interaction between education and the family in traditional, Republican, Nationalist and Communist China;

(5) to identify areas for future empirical research and identify problems and possibilities for such research;

In order to realize the above purposes, the following were the areas and related questions which would govern the development of the study:

(1) An overview of the Chinese family before 1949 in terms of the

age hierarchy and the sex hierarchy.

(2) Changes in the dominance of the age hierarchy in the modern Chinese family structure in Nationalist China on Taiwan and in Communist China on the China Mainland since 1959.

Specific questions to be answered were:

What were the changes in the family power structure in terms of age of its members, with respect to the following, related to the family in traditional China:

a. control of family finance?
b. decisions about the education of the children?
c. decisions about mate selection for the children?
d. decisions about other important family affairs, such as divisions and inheritance of family property, choice of career and profession?
e. socializing and upholding the values and ideals of the family members?
f. control of the ideology of the family members?
g. younger generation's attitude toward power in the family?

(3) Changes in dominance of the sex hierarchy in the modern Chinese family in Nationalist China and in Communist China related to the traditional family.

Specific questions to be answered were:

What were the changes in the sex hierarchy in the family with respect to the following for the female:

a. the status of the female members in the family?
b. the opportunity to receive formal education and secure gainful employment outside the family?
c. the freedom of marriage, divorce and re-marriage?
d. the equal rights to inherit family property?
e. freedom to participate in social and political activities?

Background, Significance, and Uniqueness of the Study

The Chinese family has been a very close-knit kinship structure and unit in the Chinese society for the past two thousand years and has been the place where important socialization was carried throughout the whole life, values internalized and the personality formed (16, 17, 41). The family is a very important agent in society for exercising considerable control over the individual. There is a common belief that the continuous existence and perpetuation of China and her culture for the past two thousand years shows the merit of the important functions which the Chinese family has performed (17,41). Because of those functions, the study of the changes of the Chinese family would have significance, since such changes would shape and influence the future destiny of China. And, since China is among the world powers today, especially in Asia, her future could have considerable impact on the world.

Whether Communist China can remain as a world power will depend on the cultivation of her successors of the proletarian revolution, which will further depend on the success of her education of the younger generations (11, p. 1). Since the family has exercised social, mental and moral controls over the younger generations for the past two thousand years, the Communists would have to compete with the family for the control and loyalty of the latter (41, pp. 173-174). Therefore, the Communists would try to change the family and those processes of change can be viewed as educational, social and political movements.

Having spent several years in China in the 1930's on an empirical study on the Chinese family and having therefore published the result in a book, Olga Lang pointed out the significance of the study:

> By preserving and developing the best features of their family and other human relations the Chinese can teach the rest of the world how to be faithful and devoted friends, how to respect and take care of the aged, how to enjoy the birth and growth of children, how to be tolerant and human. China needs world culture to become happy and prosperous. The world needs China to develop its civilization to the highest possible level (16, p. 346).

There were several unique features in this present study. For example, there were the following comparisons:

(1) the comparison of the age and sex hierarchy in the family in Nationalist China and Communist China with the traditional family, with special emphasis from 1959-75;

(2) the comparison of the discrepancies between the ideal and actual structures in the family in Nationalist China and Communist China, with special emphasis from 1959-75;

(3) the comparison of the relationship between education and the family in Nationalist China and in Communist China, 1959-75;

(4) the comparison of the directions of changes of the family in Nationalist China and Communist China. The former was towards the western style, yet mixed with the characteristics of the traditional family. The latter was towards the Communist model, which wanted to put the interests of the state above those of the family and individual; and uprooted and deviated from the traditional form.

Theoretical Framework

In most societies there exist the ideal as well as the real cultures. The ideal culture includes formally approved values and norms which people are supposed to follow; the real culture consists of those which they actually practice. In all societies there is a discrepancy between the ideal cultural pattern and the real cultural pattern. One common source of strain in a society is the discrepancy that sometimes exists between the ideal culture and the real culture (18, pp. 26-29).

The distinction between the ideal and actual structures is one of the most vital and useful tools of analysis of any society, any time, anywhere (18, p. 26). In this study on the changes of the modern

Chinese family, the distinction between the ideal and actual family structures were examined. Based on the theoretical propositions stated for the study of the distinctions between ideal and actual structures in society (18, pp. 26-29), the following theoretical propositions were stated for the study of the changes in the family in Nationalist China and Communist China after 1949 and used throughout the study.

1) To some extent the members of the Chinese society distinguished between the ideal and actual family structures and were aware that these did not always coincide perfectly.

2) Some of the sources of stress and strain in their family living emerged because of the discrepancies between the ideal and actual family structures in the Chinese society.

3) In the event that the strains between the ideal and actual family structures became so great, adjustments and changes would be made to integrate the two more closely.

In this study, the ideal and actual structures of kinship relations in traditional, Republican, Nationalist and Communist China were identified and examined.

The ideal and actual structures of kinship relations in traditional China were closely identical because the ideal kinship structure was supported and used by the rulers in traditional China as a mechanism to govern the people and to cultivate faithful and obedient citizens (8, p. 21). Therefore, the ideal kinship structure was actually put into practice and some of it was incorporated into laws which were enforced formally by legal sanctions and rewarded by informal social approval. The patriarchal system and filial piety are examples of that (8, p. 21; 41, pp. 5-10).

During the Republican Period between 1911-49, the ideal kinship structure of Confucius was under attack and criticism by some intellectuals and by youths and women (41, pp. 12-14). However, the Confucian kinship structure, still regarded as the ideal model was followed by many people, although with various degrees of modifications (19, p. 289). The Civil Code of 1930 was a midway compromise between the traditional and western-styled kinship structure; however, it was ahead of the custom of its time and was not enforced (41, p. 16).

The family in Nationalist China on Taiwan after 1949 has been a perpetuation of the kinship structure in the China Mainland before 1949 and based on the Civil Code of 1930 (21, p. 118). Although the Nationalist Government has not officially established an ideal model of kinship relations for the people to follow, the ideal structure of kinship relations by Confucius, with various degrees of variation and modifications, has been regarded as the model example by many people (21, pp. 117-134). However, because of the influence of the western culture, the kinship structure in Taiwan seemed to turn out to be a mixture of the Chinese and western styles, especially among the urban middle class. Therefore, the actual kinship structures in Taiwan have been in various degrees of deviations from the ideal Confucian model (21, pp. 117-134).

In Communist China, while the Communists have established an ideal socialist kinship structure for the people to follow, the traditions and customs of the Confucian kinship relations had ingrained in the life of the people for two thousand years (41, pp. 5-7). Therefore, discrepancies and strains would arise when the government tried to impose the Communist structure of kinship relations on the people against their will and customs.

Definitions of Terms

For the purpose of this study, the following terms were operationally defined.

Traditional China the social order established in the China Mainland from Confucius, 220 B.C., to the end of the Ch'ing Dynasty in 1911. It was enforced by imperial rule, sustained by an agricultural economy and composed of its basic unit-the family. The Confucian teachings and ethics were used as the basis and purpose for the continuity and stability of such a social order.

Republican China the political regime established in the China Mainland from 1911-49. The social order was sustained by a constitutional government and for the purpose of the fulfillment of the Three Principles of the People.

Nationalist China the political regime established in the island of Taiwan since 1949 by the Nationalist Party. It has perpetuated the political heritage of Republican China and based on and for the fulfillment of the Three Principles of the People.

Communist China the political regime established in the China Mainland since 1949 by the Chinese Communist Party which has based on the teachings of communism. The social order has been enforced by proletarian dictatorship, sustained by public ownership of the means of production and for the purpose of the fulfillment of a communist society.

The Family in Traditional China the kinship structure existed in traditional China based on the ethical teachings of Confucius and the "law of clan organization" by Duke Chou. Such a kinship structure was constituted by the age and sex hierarchy, family loyalty and for the purpose to continue the family heritage.

The Family in Republican China the kinship structure existed in Republican China. It was a mixture of the traditional Chinese family structure based on the ethical teachings of Confucius and the new ethical model based on the Civil Code of 1930 which was promulgated for the freedom and happiness of the individuals, especially the youths and women.

The Family in Nationalist China the kinship structure existed in Nationalist China based on the Civil Code promulgated in 1930 which is a compromise of the traditional Chinese family structure and the family structure of the West.

The Family in Communist China the kinship structure existed in Communist China based on the Marriage Law promulgated in 1950 and the ethical teachings and ideology of communism and for the purpose to support the communist revolution.

Family of Orientation the kinship group into which one is born.

Family of Procreation the kinship group formed through marriage and parenthood.

Patrilineal descent tracing of kinship through the father's family line.

Matrilineal descent tracing of kinship through the wife's family line.

Multilineal descent tracing of kinship through both the father and mother's family lines.

Patriarchal Family is one in terms of which the males take precedence over the females, other things being equal, and the family head is ideally expected to be the male sex.

Matriarchal Family is one in terms of which females are supposed to take precedence over males, and the family head is supposed to be a female.

Equalitarian Family would be one in which presumably neither males nor females took precedence over one another but shared equal powers and equal responsibilities.

Patrilocal Family residence of a married couple with the husband's parents.

Matrilocal Family residence of married couple with the wife's parents.

Neolocal Family residence of married couple separate from either set of parents.

Extended Family kinship group sharing a common residence and including a married couple, two or more of their married children, and their children's children.

Stem Family a family in terms of which one of the sons (or daughter) marries and continues to live with his parents as long as they live while all of the other sons and daughters marry and go out and join or set up other family systems.

Conjugal Family family relationships created by marriage and thus based on social rather than biological ties.

Consanquine Family family relationships that are biologically defined and based on blood ties.

Overview of Literature

Since the Chinese family has been a very important social institution in the Chinese society, it is essential to understand the family structure in traditional China and the changes in it since the Republican period. An overview of related literature will help to provide that understanding. Perhaps it is appropriate to divide these writings by the language in which they have been written, namely, in the Chinese language and English language, and by types of writings. While the family is changing, not many articles and books have been written in this area.

Literature Written in the Chinese Language

In Volume number Three of the Journal of Sociology, published by the National Taiwan University, Taipei, Taiwan in April 1967, Wen-Hui Tsai listed a bibliography of studies of the Chinese family, including articles published in Taiwan and books in Chinese available in Taiwan. Very few of them are written mainly on the family in Communist China.

Tsai also listed thirty-two books written in Chinese on the Chinese family, and twenty-two of them were published in the China Mainland before 1948 and, thus, before the Communists took over in 1949. The other ten were published in Taiwan after 1955, and only one of the ten books was written by a professional sociologist. There was a considerable number of articles in Chinese published in periodicals on the Chinese family.

The same issue of Journal of Sociology in which Tsai's bibliography appeared was devoted entirely to the family and had the following articles, surveys and research reports on the Chinese family:

"A Study of the Chinese Family Organization," by Kwan-Hai Lung and Shiao-Chun Chang.

One purpose of Lung's study was to investigate the nature of family organization among Chinese students in Taiwan. It was based upon the returns of 856 questionnaires during the years 1960-1964. The organization, power structure and family relationship were studied.

"Child Training and Child Behavior in Varying Family Patterns in a Changing Chinese Society," by Martin M. C. Yang.

The purpose of Yang's study was to investigate the changes brought on the traditional Chinese family and the changes brought out new family and occupation patterns. Child training differed somewhat in each of these categories. The data were gathered from two hundred young students in three universities in Taipei, Taiwan.

"The Statistical Analysis of Marriage and Family Problem Cases of the Taiwan Provincial Women's Association" by Polly P.Y. Ting Chi and Mei-Lien Huang.

The aim of Chi and Huang's study was to understand the reasons behind the women's problems of Taiwan and how they were handled by the Taiwan Provincial Women's Association during those recent years.

Literature Written in the English Language

There are several books written in the English language on the Chinese family by professional sociologists.

Chinese Family and Society by Olga Lang. The problems of China of the family and cultural change were the main themes of the book. She saw that the family was one of the most representative of all the Chinese social institutions in the Chinese society, and they strongly influenced each other. The scope of study covered the traditional and modern Chinese family and society, including the social institutions. Lang tried to make comparison of the two when China was in the transformation from the old to the new, from a static agrarian society into a dynamic modern society. The study was based primarily on field work carried out in China from 1935-37. The material consisted of 4,000 case histories and statistical data, 644 interviews, 1700 questionnaires, and a survey of the 26 clans. Lang used both the original source material and several historical surveys by contemporary Chinese authors who used modern scientific methods. Her study of the traditional and modern Chinese family was very complete in scope and tried to cover nearly every structure of the Chinese family, including conflict, tension and changes in the Chinese family till the 1930's. Her book was published in 1946. It is a very useful resource book in the study of the Chinese family.

Another book on the modern Chinese family published, in 1948, is The Family Revolution in Modern China by Marion Levy, Jr. This study attempted a systematic analysis of the family structure of "traditional" and "transitional" China with special reference to the role played by industrialization in the changes which were taking place. The data were obtained from materials from various written works, both European and Chinese. The secondary source was from informants, from which the bulk of the material had come, including the personal observation of the author during a year's stay in China from 1943-44. Finally, there was material derived by analysis. Perhaps the most significant contribution of his book was that the author saw that the particularistic social structure in the traditional Chinese family had extended to other social structures in society and that this extension would hinder China's development into a modern and working industrial society-a development which was already on the way.

Ten years after the Chinese Communists took over the China Mainland, a book on the Chinese family in Communist China was written by Ch'ing-K'un Yang, The Chinese Family in the Communist Revolution, published in 1959. The author was old enough to live in China when the traditional Chinese family was still in existence and saw the transition and change in the modern Chinese family. He also lived two years in the China Mainland after the Communists took over in 1949. His book was a very good resource on the traditional Chinese family, and he tried to show how the family in Communist China changed from structures of the traditional Chinese family. Yang is a Chinese himself and is a well-trained sociologist. His observations and descriptions are invaluable and authoritative. Since his book was published in 1959, the contents of the book covered only the first decade of the changes in the family in Communist China, which was then feeling the impact of the new Marriage Law.

Albert O'Hara has written about the family in Nationalist China in Taiwan. In his book Social Problem (Focus on Taiwan), the chapter on the family mainly dealt with the Chinese family in Taiwan. It touched the functions of the family in historical China, changes among Chinese university students towards marriage and the family choosing a marriage partner, divorce and adopted (foster) daughters. O'Hara has been a professor of sociology at the National Taiwan University for many years, and his book was published in May 1973. The research and studies on the changes of attitudes towards marriage and the family among university students have been the main contributions of this chapter.

There have been a few articles written covering the Chinese family from the traditional to the contemporary periods. The bibliographies of several professional journals of Asian studies have been reviewed, such as the Far Eastern Quarterly (published from 1941-1955), the Journal of Asian Studies (1956-present), The China Quarterly (1963-present), and Modern China (1975-present).

There is considerable literature on education in modern China, especially in Communist China. After the Chinese Communists took over the China Mainland in 1949, they made considerable changes in education and more significantly so after the Cultural Revolution in 1967. Changes in education in Communist China have been resulted in models significantly different from the traditional Confucian model and philosophy of education. Much attention has been focused on those changes. They were closely related with the changes on the Chinese family in the China Mainland. In Taiwan, the changes in education have been in the direction of the pattern of the west and modernization after the turn of the century, and the modern education has been the mixture of the traditional Chinese and modern western education.

Thirteen years after the Communists took over the China Mainland, a book written on the changes in education, Chinese Education Under Communism, was edited by Chang-Tu Hu, published in 1962. Education and traditional society and government, the traditional system of education, and imperial examinations were examined.

Education in Communist China by R. F. Price was published in 1970 in London. The author had special opportunity of teaching English in Peking for two years and therefore had the unique, personal experience of seeing the educational changes in Communist China, and access to many documents and resources of information which were very difficult to obtain outside China. His book covered the period up to the Cultural Revolution. This book should be regarded as a case study in the reform of education. Perhaps one of the important contributions of the book was the author's analysis of Mao Tse-Tung's thought and its impact on the reform of education in Communist China, since Mao was the chief in ruling the country. The Chinese traditional background of Mao's thought was also analyzed.

Sources and Collection of Data

The sources of data for this study included publications from professional journals, books and representative newspapers and periodicals, and interviews with potential informants. Detailed descriptions on the collection of data were given as follows:

The criteria on the sources of data were:

1) that leading and well-established journals which are accepted by professionals and professional organizations of sociology, anthropology, history and education. The data and articles should be carefully screened and for academic and scholarly credibility;

2) books which were written by prominent scholars of their own fields and were published by recognized university presses and/or well-established commercial presses should be used;

3) newspapers and periodicals which were official organs of the national governments and which thus were able to express the official opinions of the government should be used;

4) interviews with potential informants with whom the present writer was/is acquainted and which would not be of benefit to the informants.

The criteria for the selection of data also required that there be ideally, no conflicting evidences in the great majority of the data collected, but that if there were (controversies on the data), the following criteria would be used:

a) the consistency of the majority of the data would be selected over the inconsistency of some data (example: the data on the family in Nationalist China [below]).

b) the assumption that people in general prefer to be better off rather than worse off materially (18, p. 125).

Collection of the data for this study was as follows:

1. Data on the family in Traditional China (220 B.C.-1911 A.D.)

Since the family structure and education of traditional China does not exist any longer, the way chosen for this study was from the thorough review of literature and careful selection of data. Data of this study were carefully selected from leading and well-established journals and books of sociology and education and according to the criteria stated above. Most of the data were results of personal observations and life experience of the authors, plus documentary records, such as the civil code of kinship relations, the teachings of Confucius and the history of education.

Thus, there were included the most important and significant features of the traditional family structure and educational thought, such as the age hierarchy, sex hierarchy, the family as the center of loyalty and the Confucian educational thought.

2. Data on the family in Republican China (1911-1949)

Since the family structure and education of Republican China does not exist any longer, the way chosen for this study was a thorough review of literature and careful selection of data. Data of this study were carefully selected from prominent books and professional journals of sociology and education, written by professional and prominent scholars in their own fields, based on the criteria established above, such as the two books on the Chinese family written by two American sociologists, Lang and Levy, who carried on empirical studies on the Chinese family in that period. Their data included interviews, questionnaires, participant observations and official documents. The data on education were mainly collected from books written by prominent scholars in the field of education and highly recommended in professional journals.

3. Data on the family in Nationalist China (1949-present)

After a thorough study of literature and careful selection, data in the family structure in Nationalist China were collected mainly from publications of professional journals and books published by university faculty members in Taiwan, based on the criteria established above. The data of the publications of professional sociologists were based mainly on interviews, questionnaires, and participant observations. Government publications were also used since they were the only source of demographic statistics. The data on the ideal family structure were mainly collected from the government publications, such as official documents.

Concerning education, publications from the Ministry of Education were selected as they were the only source where the national educational policy and student populations could be found. The expression and interpretation of education policy were collected from the newspaper which has been the official organ of the national government. For the purpose of examining the criticism of the Nationalist Government of the Chinese students from Taiwan for studying abroad and planning to stay permanently in foreign countries, ten students from Taiwan were interviewed in Denton, Texas, in July 1975.

The data on the family in Nationalist China were collected in the first six months of 1973 when the present writer was a faculty member in a university in Taipei, Taiwan. Visits were paid to those sociologists who had publications on the family in Taiwan and appropriate materials were collected. Data have also been collected in university libraries in the U.S.A. after 1973 and up to the middle of 1975.

4. Data on the family in Communist China (1949-present)

Data on the family in Communist China were collected from the study of literature and interviews with potential informants, based on the criteria established above. As Communist China has been a totalitarian society, the government has been in control of every aspect of the people, including publications, of course. The only source of data from literature has been publications by the governments of different levels. It has been the only source where the ideal structure of the family as well as some deviations from it could be learned. As a matter of fact, the Communists openly admitted in their publications that they had not completely succeeded in changing the family, geared to their ideal family model, especially in rural areas (33, p. 7). Opposite and controversial issues and ideas were expressed and published in periodicals and newspapers. However, these would be under attacks and criticisms later on by a few editors and readers who held different viewpoints of communism (4, p. 29). Also, publications in Communist China have been centrally controlled by the national government and the principal issues and directives would be read throughout the country.

Thus the local newspapers would echo the directives from Peking. When several principal publications were obtained, the principal ideals on the changes of the Chinese family and education in Communist China could be grasped.

It is important for westerners to understand the social structure of the Chinese society so that they can have a better understanding of the family and education in China. For the past two thousand years, China was under imperial rule and the emperors had absolute power to govern the people. The common people were submissive and obedient citizens and were used to be led by their rulers (8, p. 21). Therefore, the emperors were supposed to be the parents and guardians of the common people. Even in modern China, as a custom and tradition, the government is still expected to play the leadership role.

For the purpose to collect data on the family in Communist China, the present writer spent three years as a research scholar in the Universities Service Center, Hong Kong, a well-known research center on Communist China, reviewing all the literature on the family published by the Communists. He reviewed all the literature on the family and education related to the family stored at the Universities Service Center and the Union Research Institute, which have been considered to have a very complete and comprehensive storage of the materials on Communist China. Perhaps Hong Kong is a very resourceful place to obtain publications from Communist China as it is only twenty miles away from the Chinese border. Because Hong Kong is a open society, letters and the majority of publications published in Communist China could reach Hong Kong through various channels.

Also, there are several academic centers in Hong Kong, specialized in the study of Communist China, such as the Union Research Institute, Universities Service Center, Center of Asian Studies of the University of Hong Kong, research institutes and centers in the Chinese University of Hong Kong, and the United States Information Service of the U. S. Consulate in Hong Kong. These centers have collected the first hand materials and publications in Communist China which the ordinary people could not obtain.

In order to find out the actual family structure which might deviate from the ideal structures in Communist China, the present writer interviewed four informants who had lived in Communist China in the past ten to fifteen years and whom he was/is acquainted. Because of limited financial resources, the present writer could not interview extensively in Hong Kong a large number of informants who had lived in the China Mainland before. However, he had the special opportunity in Hong Kong of associating with three teachers in a school who had left Communist China in the past few years. He gathered his data through informal conversations with them from 1970-72. Besides, he also interviewed a former Red Guard from Canton in 1972. He also interviewed a close relative who had visited the China Mainland in December of 1975. Several articles published in professional journals in the U.S.A. were included as they were empirical studies on the family in Communist China based on interviews with Chinese refugees in Hong Kong.

The principal publications both from Nationalist China and Communist China from 1957 to 1975 which were used in this study are listed as follows:

Periodicals: Chinese Youth, Chinese Women, Peking Review, The China Reconstructs, Red Flag, Peking.

Newspapers: The People's Daily, Worker's Daily, Chinese Youth Daily, Kuang Ming Daily, Peking; Southern Daily, Canton; The Central Daily News, Taipei.

Secondary data obtained by the review of professional journals such as:

The Journal of Asian Studies, published by the Association of Asian Studies, University of Michigan, Ann Arbor, Michigan.

Chinese Sociology and Anthropology, published by International Arts and Science Press, White Plains, New York.

Chinese Education, published by International Arts and Science Press, White Plains, New York.

Modern China, published by the Sage Publications, Beverly Hills, California.

The China Quarterly, published by the Contemporary China Institute of the School of Oriental and African Studies, London University, England.

Journal of Sociology, published by the Department of Sociology, National Taiwan University, Taipei, Taiwan.

Publications from the Union Research Institute, Hong Kong.

Publications from the Center of Asian Studies, University of Hong Kong, Hong Kong.

Publications from the government offices of Nationalist China, Taipei, Taiwan.

The American Sociological Review, published by the American Sociological Society, Washington, D. C.

The American Journal of Sociology, published by the Department of Sociology, University of Chicago, Chicago, Ill.

Social Forces, associated with the Southern Sociological Society, the University of North Carolina Press, Chapel Hill, North Carolina.

Journal of Marriage and the Family, published by the National Council of Family Relations, Minneapolis, Minnesota.

Recognized university presses used in this study included:

Columbia University Press
Harvard University Press
Hong Kong University Press
Massachusetts Institute of Technology Press
National Taiwan University Press
Princeton University Press

Stanford University Press
University of North Carolina Press
University of Washington Press
Yale University Press

Well-established commercial presses used in this study included:

Cheng Wen Publishing Co., Taipei, Taiwan
China Publishing Co., Taipei, Taiwan
Mei Ya Publications, Inc., Taipei, Taiwan
D. Van Nostrand Co., U.S.A.
Taiwan Commercial Press, Taipei, Taiwan
Union Research Institute, Hong Kong

Validity of Data

Based on the criteria established for the sources and collection of data, the present writer attempted to verify the validity of the data collected. A commentary on the sources of data used for a chapter is presented at the beginning of each chapter. The following is a general commentary on sources.

1) The data on the family in traditional China were collected through careful and thorough review of literature from professional journals of sociology and anthropology published in the U.S.A. and Taiwan (17, 31, 42); and several books written by sociologists and historians and published by either recognized university presses or well-established commercial presses in the U.S.A. and Taiwan (16, 20, 36). Those are authoritative and scholarly materials based on empirical investigations. Although questions were raised on the degree of adoption of the Confucian model of the traditional family by different social strata, it was agreed by scholars that the majority of the population, namely the peasants, were earnest imitators of the gentry, scholar-official classes which had strongly adopted the family structures based on the ethical teachings of Confucius and by Duke Chou (40, pp. 7, 9; 17, p. 272).

Data on the education and its relationship with the family in traditional China were collected from several books written by prominent scholars and published by either recognized university presses or well-established commercial presses in the U.S.A. or Taiwan (2, 11, 15, 20). The authors agreed that the Confucian educational thought dominated traditional China for two thousand years.

2) The data on the family in Republican China were collected from several books written by sociologists and historians and published by recognized university presses and well-established commercial presses (16, 19, 36). The authors witnessed the disintegration of the traditional family around the turn of the century. They saw the influence of the western culture on the Chinese family and different degrees of variations and modifications were observed. Two American sociologists conducted empirical studies on the Chinese family in the Republican Period and their results were published as books (16, 19).

Data on the education and its relationship with the family were collected from books written by prominent scholars and published by

15

recognized university presses or well-established commercial presses in the U.S.A. or in Taiwan (11, 15, 38) and official documents from the Ministry of Education in Republican China (22). The authors saw the collapse of the traditional educational system based on the education thought of Confucius and concerned educators tried to search for an answer to the future education in China. The influence and adoption of education of the west were observed.

3) Data on the family in Nationalist China were collected from professional journals and books of sociology and anthropology written by professionals and published by recognized university presses and well-established commercial publishers (21, 25, 31, 34, 39). The authors based their empirical studies from questionnaires, interviews and participant observations. Since most of the sociological studies used university students as samples, thus the family structure of the well-educated was studied. The studies showed significant changes and deviations from the traditional form (21, 25). On the other hand, most of the anthropological studies were done on the peasants family and their family structure have changed very little from the traditional form (37, 39). Documents from government publications were used as they are the only sources of demographic statistics of the nation (24, 35).

The following study is used as an example of using the criteria used in the collection of data when controversy existed. There was a controversy in the data on the number of divorce cases in 1965. A research reported that the number of divorce cases in Taiwan in 1965 was 265. Because the couple could sign a divorce contract in a lawyer's office, those divorce cases would not be registered with the government, or at least for a long time (25, p. 126). Therefore, the actual number of divorce cases was not known. However, according to the official document from the Nationalist Government, the number of divorce cases in 1965 was 4,840 (24, p. 1011). Besides, the number of divorce cases were 4,972 in 1969, the highest year in the late 1960's (24, p. 1011). The number of divorce cases increased each year and in 1974 it reached 6,765 cases (24, p. 1011). Because of the controversy of the data in the official document, the data from the government statistics were accepted, instead of that research.

Data on education and its relationship with the family were collected from government publications, such as from the Ministry of Education-the only source for information on student population and national educational policy (22, 23). Data were collected from a newspaper which is an official organ of the Nationalist Government and the Nationalist Party (1). Interviews were made with ten Chinese students in Denton, Texas for the purpose of discovering the relationship between education and the family, the purpose of studying abroad and staying permanently in the U.S.A. (14).

4) Data on the family in Communist China were collected from several sources. Data on the ideal structure of the family and of education with the family were collected principally from publications of the national government as it has been the only agency which can initiate and authorize such directives (3, 6, 7).

Data on the actual structure of the family and the actual structure between education and the family were collected from several sources. One of the sources has been from the publications by the Com-

16

munist Government itself. The Communist openly admitted that there are people who have not followed and adopted the values, ideology and normative patterns the national government initiated and taught (4, p. 29; 33, p. 7). On the other hand, the Communists have used their ideal model examples, articles and editorials to indoctrinate the people and constantly used examples of those who have followed and adopted their teachings to teach the people (9, 26). One possible explanation of the conflicting evidence is that many of the ideal family structure the Communists demanded the people to adopt have been in contradiction with the traditional family structure and with human nature as people prefer to be better off rather than worse off materially (18, p. 125). For example, the Communists demanded the high school and college graduates to go to the countryside to live and work with the peasants and the living conditions are difficult there. As the traditional values in China have looked down on manual labor and highly valued education (11, p. 9), many youths were reluctant to be sent there (10, p. 121) and they expressed their objections in newspapers and periodicals (5). At the same time the Communists used their hero models who were happy by obeying the Party's order to go to the countryside to persuade the people (9, pp. 24-26; 26, pp. 12-14).

Another source on the actual family structure in Communist China was from the publications in professional journals published outside Communist China (27, 32). The sources of the data from those journals were mainly based on interviews with emigrants who had left the China Mainland. Of course, those informants were dissatisfied with the Communist regime one way or another. However, interviews with the emigrants perhaps is one of the reliable sources outside Communist China.

The third source on the actual family structure in Communist China was from interviews with potential informants by the present writer. Five informants whom he interviewed are people whom he had acquainted with and those interviews did not lead to any profits or material gains to the informants. Chinese are reticent and cautious people and they would not easily trust someone whom they do not know or acquainted. So, it is necessary to get acquainted with them first and win their confidence (12, 13).

Concerning the validity of the data from Communist China as a whole, it might be a surprise to westerners that empirical investigation and studies have been widely used and adopted in Communist China. Mao Tse-Tung himself is considered as a brilliant social scientist and has already strongly emphasized the use of empirical investigation to obtain knowledge (43, pp. 119-122); especially after the Cultural Revolution in 1969 there have been drastic reforms and changes in the educational thought and philosophy. Knowledge must be obtained and based on empirical investigation and experience, and sociological ideas and interests are shared by the masses of common people (43, p. 124). Besides, the zeal for conducting social investigation has been adopted in college campuses. Students of humanities and social sciences are expected to periodically conduct social investigation in the field. The student research group should emphasize enriching their theoretical knowledge through social practice. All students must depend upon systemic survey to some extent. The result of the study is often presented in the form of a literary essay or a journalistic report. The findings are frequently shown in precise quantitative descriptions of the demographic and economic characteristics of the sampling area (43, pp. 123-

124). Therefore, the literature published in Communist China should not be treated as without accuracy, empirical basis and validity, although mixed with political indoctrinations.

Concerning the credibility of the investigator, the present writer was born and educated in Hong Kong which is still a British colony. Due to the complicated political situation of the city, the great majority of the Chinese residents there have tried to stay away from political affiliations and politics which the local government has encouraged.

The present writer was raised in Hong Kong in a family and was educated in schools which had no dieological inclination and political affiliation with the Chinese Nationalist or the Chinese Communists. He himself has no inclination to either political ideologies or affiliations with or participations in any political associations. Being a trained sociologist and an investigator in this research, he has tried to remain neutral and objective in his thought. Since he came to the U.S.A., he has still maintained his neutral political attitude towards the Chinese Nationalists and Communists.

Treatment of Data

In addition to describing the changes in the family in contemporary China, the causes of the changes were to be identified. The education of the children could be used as an example. In the traditional family, the head of the family made decisions on the education of the children as the patriarch had the power to decide everything in the family (17, p. 274). In Nationalist China today, a survey among the university students revealed that the education of children was decided upon by parents in 20 percent, parents and children together in 25 percent, and children themselves in 37 percent of the cases (21, p. 124). This change might be due to the influence of the western culture since the 1910's when the Chinese intellectuals seriously examined their own culture and searched answers from the West. The New Cultural Movement in 1917 and the May Fourth Movement in 1919 were examples of such searching (41, pp. 12-13). This self-examination and search have continued and intensified in Taiwan while it has been under the military protection of the U.S.A. The presence of the Americans, mass communications, and the contact through the educational institutions have intensified individual freedom and choice.

In Communist China, the education of the youth has been taken away from the hand of the parents. Before the Cultural Revolution started in 1966, university admissions was based on family class background and academic achievements (7, p. 19). After the Cultural Revolution in 1967, university admission has been based on the working unit to which a youth belonged. He would be recommended by his unit to enter the university based on his performance shown from his enthusiasm in work, and the recommendation and approval from his working unit and the people (30). Obviously, this change was generated by the Communists, and the cause was easily identified.

Divorce was a significant item to be used for comparison. In the traditional Chinese family, divorce was very rare. The married couple had to endure the hardship of their unhappy marriage, sometime for the rest of their lives because a marriage united not only two persons, but

18

two families (41, pp. 64-67). In Nationalist China, there were 6,765 divorce cases recorded by the government in 1974 with a population of 16 million (24, p. 1011) as divorce is permitted in the Civil Code promulgated in 1930 (34, pp. 141-194). The main cause for divorce were bigamy, adultery, bad treatment by spouse and relatives (25, p. 126). In Communist China, divorce cases have been handled by the local or district government and the number of divorce cases increased drasticly after the promulgation of the Marriage Law (28). Most of the people who sought divorce were in their early twenties and were married under the new Marriage Law. They got married in a hurry and when they could not get along in a few months, they sought a divorce (29).

Comparison could be made on the number, form and causes of divorce in the family in traditional, Nationalist and Communist China.

Development of the Study

Chapters I to III are the foundations of this study. Chapter I has been the introduction and has included the theoretical framework, data collection, and the uniqueness and significance of this study. Chapter II consists of an overview of the characteristics of the traditional Chinese family which are used as the basis for comparison to identify changes in the family away from that tradition in Nationalist China and Communist China. Chapter III describes the changes away from the traditional family in Republican China, with special emphasis on the age and sex hierarchy.

Chapters IV to VII examine the changes away from traditional family in the age and sex hierarchy in the family in Nationalist China and Communist China with respect to the ideal and actual structures. In the age hierarchy changes concerning the decisions on the children's education, career, marriage and the status of the head of the family are examined. In the sex hierarchy, the status of women and the opportunity to receive formal education, secure gainful employment outside the family, freedom of marriage, divorce and remarriage are examined.

Chapters VIII to X examine the relationship and interaction between education and the family in China. The Confucian school of educational thought dominated the education in traditional, Republica, and Nationalist China, and education was supported by the rulers and monopolized by the upper and upper-middle classes. In Communist China the Communists have tried to reverse such a tradition and make education to serve and to be controlled by the proletariat.

Chapter XI is the conclusion of the study. The whole study is summarized and changes on the age and sex hierarchy of the family in modern China are discussed, with respect to the ideal and actual structures. Suggestions for further studies are given.

BIBLIOGRAPHY--CHAPTER I

1. Taipei, <u>Central Daily News</u>, May 6, 16, 27, June 1, 8, 9, 11 1975; May 22, 1976.

2. Chang, Chung-Li, <u>The Chinese Gentry</u>, Seattle, University of Washington Press, 1967. 3rd printing.

3. Chang, Ta-Pang, "Use The Revolutionary Life Viewpoint to Face the Problems of Love," <u>Chinese Women</u>, May 1, 1964. Peking. 27-28.

4. "Should Not Mistreat and Abandon Your Parents," editorial, <u>Chinese Youth</u>, (December 1, 1956), 29.

5. "Dilemma of Youth: What Do They Want Us to Do, Work or Study?" <u>Chinese Youth</u>, Peking, (April 16, 1965), NTIS.

6. Peking, <u>Chinese Youth Daily</u>, May 28, 1964.

7. Chu, Yen, "Why the University Enrolling System Should Be Reformed," <u>Peking Review</u>, (September 21, 1973), 19-21.

8. Fan, Jo-Yu, "Why We Abolished the Feudal Patriarchal System," <u>Red Flag</u> (Hung Ch'i) Peking, (March 1, 1960), 19-27.

9. Fang, Yu, "Breaking the Family Bondage and Becoming A Good Child of the Proletariat," <u>Chinese Youth</u>, (November 1, 1964), 24-26.

10. Hong Kong Government Press, <u>Hong Kong 1973</u>, <u>Report of Year 1972</u>.

11. Hu, Chang-Tu, ed. <u>Chinese Education Under Communism</u>, New York, Teacher's College, Columbia University, 1962.

12. Interviewed with three educated refugees in Hong Kong, 1972-1972.

13. Interviewed with a former Red Guard, Hong Kong, October 1972.

14. Interviewed with ten Chinese students in Denton, TX, July 1975.

15. Jen, Shih-Hsien, <u>The History of Chinese Educational Thought</u>, Taipei, Taiwan Commercial Press, 1972, 4th ed.

16. Lang, Olga, <u>Chinese Family and Society</u>, Yale University Press, 1946. Archon Books, 1968.

17. Lee, Shu-Ching, "China's Traditional Family, Its Characteristics and Disintegration," <u>American Sociological Review</u>, XVIII (June 1953), 272-280.

18. Levy, Marion J. Jr., <u>Modernization and the Structure of Societies</u>, Princeton University Press, 1966.

19. Levy, Marion J. Jr., <u>The Family Revolution in Modern China</u>, Cambridge, Harvard University Press, 1949.

20. Li, Dun J., _The Essence of Chinese Civilization_, Princeton, D. Van Nostrand Co., 1967.

21. Lung, Kwan-Hai and Shiao-Chun Chang, "A Study of the Chinese Family Organization," _Journal of Sociology_, No. 3, April 1967, National Taiwan University, 117-134.

22. Ministry of Education, Republic of China, _Education in the Republic of China_, Taipei, The Veteran Printing Press, 1970.

23. Ministry of Education, Republic of China, _Educational Statistics of the Republic of China_, 1973. Taipei, Taiwan, 1973.

24. Ministry of the Interior, Republic of China, _1974, Taiwan-Fukien Demographic Fact Book, Republic of China_, Taipei, Taiwan, 1975.

25. O'Hara, Albert R., _Social Problems: Focus on Taiwan_, Taipei, Taiwan, Mei Ya Publications, Inc. 1973.

26. Pai, Chi-Hsien, "Integration with the Poor and Lower-Middle Peasants," _Peking Review_, July 26, 1974, 12-14.

27. Parrish, William L. Jr., "Socialism and the Chinese Peasant Family," _Journal of Asian Studies_, Vol. XXXIV, No. 3, May 1975, 613-630.

28. Peking, _People's Daily_, October 31, 1951.

29. Peking, _People's Daily_, March 7, 1957.

30. Peking, _People's Daily_, March 4, 1972.

31. Ruey, Yih-Fu, "Changing Structure of the Chinese Family," _Journal of Archaeology and Anthropology_, XVII, XVIII (November, 1961), 1-15.

32. Salaff, Janet W., "The Emerging Conjugal Relationship in the People's Republic of China," _Journal of Marriage and the Family_, November 1973, 705-717.

33. Soong, Ching-Ling, "Women's Liberation in China," _Peking Review_, February 11, 1972, 6-7.

34. Tai, Yen-Fai, _The Family Law of China_, Cheng Wen Printing Co., November 1970. 6th Ed.

35. Taiwan Provincial Labor Force Survey and Research Institute, _Quarterly Report of the Labor Force Survey in Taiwan, Republic of China_, No. 50, Taipei, Taiwan, January 1976.

36. T'ao, Hsi-Sheng, _Marriage and Kins_, Taipei, Taiwan Commercial Press, 1968. 2nd ed.

37. Ting, Polly P.Y. Chi and Mei-lein Huang, "The Statistical Analysis of Marriage and Family Problem Cases of the Taiwan Provincial Women's Association," _Journal of Sociology_, National Taiwan University, Taipei, April 1967, 137-152.

21

38. Wang, Yi-Chu, _Chinese Intellectuals and the West, 1872-1949_. Chapel Hill, University of North Carolina Press, 1966.

39. Wolf, Margery, _Women and the Family in Rural Taiwan_, Stanford, Stanford University Press, 1972.

40. Wong, Aline Kan, _Changes in the Marriage and Family Institutions in China, 1949-1969_, working paper of the seminar on Social Change in China, Center of Asian Studies, The University of Hong Kong, Hong Kong, May 2, 1970.

41. Yang, Ch'ing-K'un, _Chinese Communist Society: The Family and the Village_, M.I.T. Press, 1972, 5th printing, copyright 1959.

42. Yang, Martin M.C., "Child Training and Child Behavior in Varying Family Patterns in a Changing Chinese Society," _Journal of Sociology_, III (April, 1967), National Taiwan University, 77-83.

43. Young, L.C., "Mass Sociology: The Chinese Style" _The American Sociologists_, Vol. 9, 1974, pp. 117-125.

CHAPTER 2

AN OVERVIEW OF THE TRADITIONAL FAMILY BEFORE 1911

This chapter is used as a foundation for comparing the changes in the family in Nationalist China and in Communist China. Since the traditional Chinese family does not exist any longer, the way chosen for this study was from the thorough review of literature and careful selection of data.

The data of this chapter were collected from three sources. Data from the U.S.A. included four books and two articles. Two of the books were written by two professional sociologists (6, 16) and one book was written by a professional anthropologist (4). All three were published by recognized university presses. One book is a selected translation of the essence of the Chinese civilization and was published by a well-established commercial press (8). The two articles were published in two professional journals of sociology (1, 7).

The data from Nationalist China on Taiwan included two books and three articles. One book on the family law of China was written by a well-known former professor of law now the President of the Judicial Yuan (cabinet) (14), and the other book was written by a well-known social scientist (15). Both books were published by well-established presses in Taiwan. The three articles were written by a sociologist (17) and an anthropologist (12, 13) and were published in the professional journals of sociology and anthropology of a recognized university press.

The data from Communist China on the China Mainland included five articles from three periodicals which are official organs of the Communist Government (2, 3, 9, 10, 11).

The data from the United States, Nationalist China, and Communist China do not conflict with respect to the major characteristics of the traditional family, although each one takes a different viewpoint to analyze the data. The data collected from the U.S.A. showed an objective and neutral position to examine the traditional Chinese family. The data from Nationalist China often showed the strength of the traditional family and avoided mention of its weaknesses. It was perhaps due to the political and social situation in Taiwan since the ethical teachings of Confucius were respected and honored by high-ranking government officials, the older generation, and in educational institutions. The data from Communist China showed an antagonistic position, since the Communists have planned to establish a communist model of the family which has been in conflict of interest with the traditional family.

Since this chapter includes the data from the U.S.A., Nationalist China and Communist China, different viewpoints were included. However, the present writer relied heavily on the data from the U.S.A., as they were provided by professional scholars and appeared in publications of recognized university presses, well-established commercial presses, and professional journals. Besides, they took a neutral and objective position to analyze the traditional family, being less likely to be influenced by political forces.

The traditional Chinese family was modeled after the "law of clan organization" by Duke Chou and the ethical teachings of Confucius in the fifth century B.C. It lasted for the following two thousand years because the rulers of traditional China found it useful for the purpose of ruling the country and for the cultivation of faithful civil servants and obedient citizens, as well as for the creation of a peaceful and stable society (3, pp. 19-23).

There were several significant and unique characteristics of the traditional family in historical China. They were the dominance of the sex hierarchy (the emphasis on the father-son relationship), the dominance of the age hierarchy (the patriarchal system), the family as the center of loyalty, the cult of ancestor worship (which yielded the by-product, conservatism), and the encouragement of the large family (an ideal practiced only by the wealthy minority). These five characteristics constituted most of the significant features of the traditional family. They are used in this study as the basis for comparison with the family in contemporary China, to identify, as much as possible, changes in ideal and actual structures. Although the degrees of acceptance of these normative patterns might vary within different social classes, the more wealthy, prestigious, established, and educated a class was, the more would be the degree of internalization and acceptance (7, p. 272). The family of the gentry and official-dom was considered as the model in traditional China, and the peasants were earnest imitators of the life pattern established by the gentry-scholar class (7, p. 272).

Before the period of Confucius, there were few and only limited written records on the family, in the period of game hunting and cattle breeding and primitive agriculture, but the family seems to have been quite different from that found after the period of Confucius (12, pp. 1-3, 9). The following historical view is limited to the period following Confucius (551-479 B.C.) who prescribed the pattern of the traditional family. A brief historical overview of the main characteristics of the traditional family follows.

Dominance of the Sex Hierarchy

The dominance of the male members in the family in traditional China began from the Chou Dynasty (1100-220 B.C.). The economy shifted from game hunting and cattle breeding, which had been managed by women. Agriculture was later taken over by men. Men thus became the heads of the families, and women became their dependents. In agriculture, collective as well as divided labor was needed, and family organization began to emerge (15, pp. 19-20).

It was first "the law of clan organization" (the institution of Tsung-fa) that defined the social structure of the traditional Chinese family. It was traditionally attributed to Duke Chou. It was elaborated by Confucius and his followers to maintain clan solidarity. In the clan, the line of descent had to be patrilineal; it was father-right in which status, office, privileges, property, etc., would be passed from the father to the sons; it was patriarchal in that the oldest male member in a clan had the power to rule and control; it was primogeniture in that the eldest or selected son had priority over his younger brothers in the transmission of hereditary titles, and the primogenitary line had priority over collateral lines in family descent; it was patrilocal in that the married sons had to live with their parent or parents; it was exogamous in that and marriage within the clan was forbidden (12, p. 3). Although "the law of clan organization" was mainly for the kinship structure of the noble class, it was adopted in various forms, after the Chou Dynasty, as a model of kinship structure.

Emphasis on the Father-Son Relationship

It will be helpful to use an example in history to illustrate the importance of father-son relationship. The incident was recorded by Suu-Ma Ch'ien, a well-known Chinese historian in the second century B.C., in his Historical Records (Shih Chi), roll 39, "The State of Hsin" (8, p. 362). In the fifth year of Duke Hsien's reign (672 B.C.), the Duke attacked Li-jung, a non-Chinese tribe, and defeated the enemy and acquired Madame Li and her younger sisters who later became the Duke's favorite concubines. In the twelfth year (665 B.C.) Madame Li gave birth to a son named Hsi-Ch'i, and the Duke began to think seriously of replacing Shen-Sheng, an eldest son, with Hsi-Ch'i as the crown prince (8, p. 362).

In the seventeenth year (660 B.C.) of his reign, the Duke ordered crown prince Shen-Sheng to lead an army to attack Tung-shan, a non-Chinese tribe (8, p. 362). He talked to Li K'e, a minister, saying that he could not decide which one of his sons should be his heir apparent. Li K'e did not reply, but later went to see Shen-Sheng, who asked if he would be replaced as the crown prince. The minister then told him that he should do his best to command the army and that as long as he was respectful to his father, he should not be worried about being replaced as the crown prince. He further advised him that he should be more concerned to be a loyal son than to be the heir apparent. He would be safe if he diligently cultivated his virtue (8, p. 362).

In the nineteenth year (658 B.C.), the Duke told Madame Li privately that he intended to replace Shen-Sheng with Hsi-Ch'i as the crown prince. She protested in tears, saying that Shen-Sheng was known throughout the country, was the head of the army, and that it was wrong to replace the eldest son of a legal wife by the young son of a concubine. She threatened to commit suicide if the Duke insisted on the replacement (8, p. 363).

Although Madame Li had praised the crown prince outwardly, in secret she wished her son to become the crown prince. One day, in the twenty-first year (656 B.C.), Madame Li told the crown prince that she had dreamed about Madame Chiang, the crown prince's deceased mother, and she asked the crown prince to offer sacrifice in Ch'ufu to comfort his deceased mother. After the ritual of sacrifice, the crown prince brought back the sacrificial meat to his father as tribute. The Duke was hunting outside the capitol, and Madame Li ordered her servants to put poison in the meat (8, p. 363).

25

Two days later the Duke returned from his hunting trip and the royal chef presented the sacrificial meat. When the Duke was ready to eat, he was stopped by Madame Li who said that the meat should be tested first as it had come from a far distance. The Duke threw it on the ground, and the ground began to bulge. When a dog and a slave ate the meat, both died instantly. Then Madame Li said in tears how cruel the prince was in trying to kill his own father, threatened to flee with her son before it was too late, and she regretted that she had opposed replacing Shen-Sheng with her son (8, p. 363).

When the crown prince had heard about the plot of Madame Li to accuse him, he immediately fled to Hsinch'eng. Unable to arrest the crown prince, the Duke was very furious and killed the tutor of the prince for substitute (8, p. 363).

Someone told the crown prince that the poison was placed by Madame Li and that he should tell his father about his innocence. But the crown prince said that the Duke was very old and needed Madame Li for his old age. If he had told the Duke the truth, the latter would have been very angry with Madame Li, and the prince did not want his father to be troubled in his old age. Someone suggested that the prince flee to another state, but the prince replied that no state would accept him as a guest since he had such a bad reputation, and that the only way out for him was to commit suicide. On the Wushen day of the Twelfth Month, Crown Prince Shen-Sheng committed suicide at Hsinch'eng (8, p. 363).

From this incident one can see the father-right, in which the status, office, privileges, property, etc., would be passed from the father to the sons. Also, there is primogeniture, in which the eldest son or selected successor had priority over his younger brothers in the transmission of hereditary titles. Also, the filial piety of the crown prince can be seen.

A more recent example of the father-son relationship is provided in the following letter of Tseng Kuo-Fan (1811-1872) to his son Chi-Tseh (8, p. 348). Tseng was a very famous military general and official in the Ch'ing Dynasty.

To Chi-tseh, the 4th day of the 3rd (leap) month, 1860
     Your letter of the 16th was received on the first day of the month.
     Since Uncle Ch'eng has moved to the new residence, you are now the lord of our old homestead, the Golden House. My grandfather, the honorable Hsing-Kang, attached great importance to the successful management of the household. First, he insisted that every member of our family should get up early in the morning. Second, the house should be washed and swept regularly to keep it clean. Third, the offering of sacrifice to the deceased ancestors should be performed in the most sincere manner. Fourth, all of our neighbors, relatives and clan members should be well treated. Whenever they came to our house, they were always received with great respect. We gave them financial help if they were in need. We offered them our good offices if they were involved in lawsuits; congratulated them on wedding and other festivals

occasions; provided comfort when they were sick; and sent them condolences after the death of any of their family members.

Besides the four items described above, the honorable Hsing-Kang paid constant attention to the study of books and the raising of vegetables. Recently when I wrote letters home, I often reminded you of the importance of "books, vegetables, fish, and hogs." I want you to know that whenever I did this, I merely followed the tradition established by my grandfather.

Now that you are busy pursuing your studies, you may feel that you are not able personally to supervise all of the eight activities described above. But in any case you should understand the meaning behind these activities. Ask Mr. Chu-su (a family steward) to be particularly careful in this matter because all of these activities are extremely important. As for the sacrificial ceremonies, tell your mother that she should have them in mind constantly. Only the best food and vessels can be used for the purpose of offering sacrifices. A family's fortune cannot last long if the family is not particular when offering sacrifices, no matter how prosperous it is at the moment. Remember this! (8, p. 351).

The Status and Roles of Women

The emphasis on the father-son relationship affected the status and roles of women in the traditional family, especially in marriage, divorce, and remarriage. As a child, a girl received parental affections and material benefits as did her brother. The first discrimination would come in the opportunity for education. The opportunity would go to the male members of the family and to her brothers first, since she was considered a liability to the family in that she would leave it after her marriage (16, p. 106). There was a common belief and proverb that "a woman without talent is virtuous." In some wealthy families, private tutors were hired to teach the girls, but in general, the girl was taught by her mother to do house work and thus to prepare her to be a wife and obedient daughter-in-law (6, p. 47).

A girl's most difficult time came after her marriage, which was arranged by her parents and before which she had little knowledge of, or acquaintance with, her future spouse. She entered into a new family and had to serve her mother-in-law, particularly, who was in charge of instructing the new daughter-in-law to fit into the regulations of the family (16, p. 106). There were descriptions and norms for how a daughter-in-law in the traditional family should behave. In the Ching Dynasty, a man named Lu Ch'i-Ch'i wrote a "Young Wife's Guide" for brides:

The new bride's world consists of her father-in-law, her mother-in-law, and her husband and no others; she must satisfy their wishes and not cross them in the slightest.
Before her father- and mother-in-law arise, the bride must first wash and comb herself quickly and without dallying so that as soon as her in-laws awake she may go to ask their health and wish them well. She must make the

three meals each day herself and at the time of serving
food, stand to one side and assist those who are eating...
if there are young animals, she must drive them outside...
In the evening if the master is at home, even if she re-
ceives permission to retire early to her room, she must
quietly do her woman's work and may not go to sleep too
early. If the master is not at home, she must wait until
her mother-in-law retires and then set things in order and
go to her room (3, p. 24).

What is the "guide for satisfying the wishes of her husband?" The
author said:

> Just after being married, the bride must stand up
> even when she sees her husband far away. If she remains
> quietly seated, she is a vain and disrespectful wife. Af-
> ter quietly and briefly greeting him, she must refer to him
> respectfully, such as 'young master' and 'respectful hus-
> band' and may not refer to him as 'you'...Whenever she of-
> fers food and tea, she must make obeisance with both hands
> and serve with a modest demeanor; she must bring forth warm
> clothing before it is yet cold and bring out the food be-
> fore her husband is famished...Every morning, she must pay
> her respects ceremoniously; when her husband comes home
> from far away, she must make two obeisance from the attic
> window." (3, p. 24).

There were certain popular social norms still often heard about
even in the contemporary Chinese society outside Communist China today.
There are the "three cardinal guidance principles and five constant
virtues" and the "three obediences and four virtues."

The "three cardinal guidance" principles meant that the monarch
guides the subject, the father guides the son, and the husband guides
the wife (2, p. 6). The "five constant virtues" are the principles of
benevolence, righteousness, propriety, wisdom, and fidelity (2, p. 6).
The "three obediences," means that a young girl should obey her father
in the family, that a married woman should obey her husband, and that a
widow should obey her son (2, p. 6). The "four virtues" are women's
virtues, speech, appearance, and work. Specifically, "women's virtue"
means that a woman should know her place and act in compliance with the
ethical code. "Women's speech" means that a woman should not talk too
much. "Women's appearance" means that a woman should adorn herself to
please her husband. "Women's work" means that a woman must do all her
household work well and willingly (2, p. 6).

When a married woman gave birth to a son, her status was improved
in the family, since she had fulfilled the purpose of perpetuating the
family lineage. As her children grew older, her status and authority
in the family grew even stronger. When she was a grandmother, she was
the most powerful woman in the family, ranking next to her husband in
status, were he still alive (16, p. 106). Since marriage in traditional China was for the purpose of perpetuation of family lineage of the
husband's family and for the service of the parents-in-law, a wife
could be repudiated by her parents-in-law if she could not fulfill the
purpose of the marriage. There were actually seven reasons that a husband could divorce his wife but the wife could not, however, divorce

the husband. A wife could be repudiated by her husband because she:
(1) disobeyed her husband's parents, (2) failed to bear children, (3)
committed adultery, (4) exhibited jealousy, (5) had some repulsive disease, (6) was garrulous, (7) stole (12, p. 6). But she could not be
sent away if (1) she had mourned her husband's parents for three years,
(2) her husband's family had become wealthy, (3) she had no family to
take her in (12, p. 6).

It was from the T'ang Dynasty (618-906 A.D.) to the Ch'ing Dynasty
(1644-1911 A.D.) that a wife could be repudiated for the above seven
reasons and for three reasons could not be divorced. The seven reasons
of repudiation were based on the interests of ancestral lineage, the
parents-in-law, and the family and clan, and were not based on the interest of the husband (14, p. 147). However, because marriage in traditional China cost a large amount of money, only the wealthy family
could afford a divorce and, thus, a new marriage. Also, the objection
and interference of the wife's family, particularly if it was a wealthy
and powerful one and the judgement of public opinions could prevent
the husband's family from repudiating the wife (14, p. 147).

In the Code of the T'ang, Sung, Ming and Ch'ing Dynasties, divorce
by consent of both husband and wife existed. A divorce by consent
could be obtained if the husband and wife could not get along, if the
husband could not find one of the seven reasons to repudiate the wife,
if the husband did not want to make known in public one of the seven
reasons for divorce, if the wife could not stand mistreatment by her
husband, or if her family could not return the bethrothal gift to the
husband (14, pp. 147-148).

Forced divorce by law also existed in the Code to T'ang, Ming and
Ch'ing Dynasties. The married couples would be punished if they did
not dissolve their marriage if it was decided by the court that they
should do so. The court would order a forced divorce if (1) the husband beat the grandparents and/or parents of the wife, killed her close
relatives, or committed adultery with his mother-in-law; (2) if the
wife beat and/or scolded the grandparents of the husband, injured his
relatives, committed adultery with his older generations, and/or attempted to murder her husband; (3) if the older generations of the married couple killed one another (14, p. 148).

In traditional China, a widow was prevented from remarriage because
of the mores of chastity which required a woman to be married to only
one husband for her whole life. If the widow insisted upon leaving the
family of her deceased husband and upon remarrying, she could not take
her children and family property. Considering social pressures against
one marrying a widow, she could hardly find any good chance for remarriage (16, p. 65). Cheng Yi demanded that women should keep their chastity, saying that "starving to death is insignificant, while loss of
chastity is a great matter." Remarriage of a widow was a loss of chastity (9, p. 18).

The destiny of a widow was "doom" in traditional China. While a
widow was legally allowed to remarry, the fact that she could not take
her children and property with her usually led her to choose widowhood
in order to raise her children. Committing suicide was a way out for
those widows whose future destiny was uncertain, as when having no children to raise, being too old to remarry, or having a strong moral aver-

sion to remarriages. In the traditional Chinese society, the suicide of such a widow was praised (8, p. 386). The virtue of widowhood which society praised had a high price of pretense for the widow to pay as against her wishes. Some widows even committed suicide because they were aware of the hardships a widow had to suffer (8, p. 392).

However, Chou Chi, a scholar of the Ch'ing Dynasty, criticized the imposition of permanent widowhood in society upon widows who wished to remarry, but who declined doing so because of children. Chou suggested that a widow should be allowed to maintain relationship with her children even after she remarried. Thus, a widow would not be forced by her parents-in-law to continue her widowhood; in case she chose to continue her widowhood, it would be voluntary and genuine (8, p. 392). Chou's opinion could hardly have any impact on such a social tradition, however.

The Dominance of the Age Hierarchy

The dominance of the older generation, the parent in particular, over the younger generation, namely the children, was a significant characteristic of the traditional family. The head of the family, the patriarch, usually a male, was the eldest and the chief economic producer in the family. Since the family was the basic economic unit in historical China, the patriarchal system was needed to manage the production in the family. The patriarch was responsible for payment of rent and taxes, and the responsibilities of the family to state and to society were shouldered by him also (3, pp. 19-21). In this section, in order to illustrate the dominance of the older generation in the traditional family, the following items will be examined: (1) the stratification by the age hierarchy in the kinship system, (2) the patriarchal system and filial piety and, finally, (3) the dominance of the parents in children's marriage.

The Stratification by the Age Hierarchy in the Kinship System

The dominance of the older generation over the younger was an explicit characteristic in the traditional family and was still predominant in the early Republic era. The age hierarchy was determined by generation, age and proximity of kinship and was the structure for status and authority in the traditional Chinese family and kinship circle. Relatives in a senior generation enjoyed higher status and authority than did those in a junior generation. Older members in the same generational level preceded the younger ones. Relatives who were closer in kinship, senior in generational level, and older in chronological age had more status and authority (16, pp. 87-89). The hierarchy of status and authority forced an individual to observe his own place in the kinship structure through mores of filial piety, social pressure, and sanction within the kinship circle. Filial piety demanded complete obedience, submission, and devotion to parents and was fully supported by law in the Ching Dynasty before 1912 and by informal coercion by the clan regulations in rural areas even in the 1950's (16, p. 89). In addition to social coercion, parental affection and parent-child interdependence were important mechanisms causing children to observe filial piety and creating in them a feeling of gratitude toward their parent

(16, p. 90).

The Patriarchal System and Filial Piety

Filial piety in the traditional family meant that the parents occupied the first and the most important position in the children's
minds. The interest of the parents had the first priority (1, p. 51).
The traditional filial piety demanded even deeper relationship between
the father and his son: "It is an act of integrity for a father to
cover up the mistakes of his son and for a son to cover up the misdeed
of his father." That was written by Confucius in his Book of Analects
(10, p. 23). In the traditional society as well as in modern Chinese
society today (outside Communist China), there were few universal pen-
sion systems established for the retired or disabled senior citizens in
their old age, and the family was the unit of economic production and
consumption. Therefore, parents had to count on their children, particularly sons, to provide them with support in their old age. As a
popular Chinese proverb says, "raise children for the support in the old
age and to accumulate grains for the famine."

Lang examined the relationship structure within the nuclear family.
She observed the hierarchy of status and authority operating according
to generation, age, and sex. The head of the family, such as the father, had enormous power. As the official head and representative of the
family, he was in control of family property, and he determined the
children's education, career, marriage, and the destiny of the family.
If the father died or was unable to take care of the family, the eldest
son became the head of the family (6, p. 43). If the eldest son was
too young, the mother became the authority and would bring up the children (6, p. 29).

The patriarchal system first came into existence in the feudal
period three thousand years ago when the family first began to exist as
the basic economic unit of the feudal society. Under the economic situation of small scale production, the peasant family combined their
primary economic activity - agriculture - with subsidiary handicraft
industry and carried on production by the family unit. The landlord
family owned pieces of land and exploited the surplus labor of the
peasants, who rented the field for production. The peasant family also
worked on a small piece of its own farmland (3, pp. 19-20). However,
the state government and the landlords wanted to have the guarantee
that the peasant would pay their taxes and rents, and a head of the
family, namely the patriarch was established to take up this responsibility. Besides, in order to guarantee sufficient labor power for
themselves, the landlord class utilized family relationship among the
peasants as the principal method for binding the peasants to the land.

The head of the family also bore other legal responsibilities of
the family and its members. The patriarch had the authority to educate,
discipline, and punish other family members. The patriarch was made
the absolute ruler in the family because the landlord class and feudal
rulers wanted to make use of the patriarch to exercise political and
economic control over the peasant family, and they thus made the family
a political and economic unit (3, p. 21). As the Book of Rites says,
"While one's parents are alive, a person will have no private property".

The patriarch also had the duty and authority to educate the family members to perpetuate the virtues and good conduct of ancestors and to regulate the members of the family and the clan to observe the laws of the state and rules of the family and the clan (7, pp. 274-275). He had to officiate at all the important and sacrificial ceremonies of the family (5, pp. 133-134). Since the head of the family had the legal responsibility in society, the whole family would get involved if one of its members committed serious criminal offenses, such as treason to the state. Punishment might extend to the families of a person's father, mother and wife (15, pp. 66-67).

The patriarch was also the guardian of family property. From the T'ang Dynasty (618-906 A.D.) the head of the family had absolute authority to control and manage the family property and to approve and supervise the younger generations in the management of it. However, family property belonged to the proper heirs in the family and was to be fairly divided among the heirs. Otherwise, the patriarch would be guilty of a criminal offense (15, pp. 90-91).

A letter from Tseng Kuo-Fan to his son illustrates the duty of the patriarch to his family members:

To Chi-tseh, the 14th day of the 10th month, 1859
    I received your letters of the 19th and the 29th and learned that the wedding had taken place. It is fortune of our family that your newly married wife has learned to endear herself to your mother.
    For more than two hundred years the emperors of our dynasty have had the habit of getting up at the yin hour (from 4 to 6 A.M.). The forebears of our family established a similar tradition. Both the honorable Ching-hsi and the honorable Hsing-kang had the habit of getting up before daybreak. In winter time they got up and sat for two hours before daylight appeared. My father, the honorable Chu-t'ing, got up every morning as soon as there was daylight. He would not wait for daybreak if there was something important that had to be taken care of. You must have observed this yourself.
    Recently I have also formed the habit of getting up as soon as the day breaks, in the hope that I shall be able to continue the tradition of our forebears. Now that you have reached adulthood and have been married, the first thing you should remember and devote yourself to is getting up early each morning. You should set an example to your newly married wife and urge her to do likewise.
    Throughout my life my main shortcoming has been the lack of perseverance, and consequently I have not been able to achieve anything worthwhile. I have not succeeded in the establishment of virtues nor the accomplishment of good deeds; I am deeply ashamed. (This remark came from a man who, more than anyone else, was responsible for the suppression of the Tai-ping Rebellion and thus saved the Ch'ing dynasty for another fifty years.) Since I began to manage military affairs, I have not had the time to devote myself to other subjects. I frequently change my mind about what I really want to do; this is a good indication of my lack of perseverance, for which I feel a strong sense of shame

within myself. If you wish to accomplish something in your life, you should begin with the word "perseverance".

From my observation of the honorable Hsing-kang, I have concluded that his extraordinary mannerism can be summarized in one word: dignity. I have followed his example and I believe that my mannerism, whether in sitting or in walking, is also a dignified one. One of your main shortcomings is that you are too flippant in your manners. From now on you should watch yourself at all times with regard to this matter. You should be serious and dignified, whether you are sitting or walking.

In summary, these three requirements - early rising, perseverance, and dignity - are most important to you at the moment. Early rising is our family tradition; the lack of perseverance is one of my worst shortcomings of which I am greatly ashamed; and the lack of dignity is a shortcoming of yours. I cannot possibly overemphasize these words (8, pp. 350-351).

Parental Arrangement of Children's Marriages

The significance of the dominance of the age hierarchy in the traditional family is exemplified in the parental arrangement of and dominance of the children's marriage. Marriage has been a very important event in a person's life in the Chinese family for the formation of a life-long partnership. The parental arrangement and dominance in the children's marriages fully revealed the dominance and pressure of the age hierarchy. It supported familism, putting the interests of the family above those of the individuals.

The patriarch had the duty and authority to arrange his children's marriage in order to perpetuate the family lineage and to serve the ancestor's temple (3, pp. 22-23). The conditions of mate selection applied mainly to the future daughter-in-law since the purpose of marriage was for the family of the husband to serve the ancestor in the temple and to perpetuate the coming generation (14, p. 6). Therefore, to choose a future daughter-in-law, the man's parents would consider a prospective wife in terms of her capability to bear children, of compliance with the family's traditions and rules, and of ability to carry household drudgery. Also, the parents would consider whether the future daughter-in-law could get along with her future family members (7, p. 276). The new daughter-in-law would be required to serve her future parents-in-law (16, p. 23). In the lower class family, women were required to participate in farming and physical labor to help family finance (3, p. 25).

The dominance of the older generation can be seen from Ssu Ma-Kuang's "Family Manners":

All sons serve their mothers and fathers, all wives serve their in-laws. Before it is light they rise, wash themselves, comb their hair, and put on their hairdress. Just before dawn, they go to their parents' and in-laws' room to await their pleasure. When the parents and in-laws arise, the sons present the medicine, the wives, with proper modesty, pay their respects and then withdraw, each to their

own work. The sons and their wives ask what the head of
the family wishes to eat and bring it to him. Having respectively offered chopsticks, the sons and their wives
then withdraw and themselves eat. The husband and their
wives each seat themselves in their own places according
to their age... In the evening when the parents and in-laws
wish to retire, they set everything in order and then withdraw. When they have nothing to do, they attend their parents and in-laws outside their rooms; their attitude must
not venture to make a sound near their parents and in-laws;
when their parents and in-laws do not order them to sit,
they may not attempt to sit down; if they are not ordered
to leave, they may not leave (3, p. 24).

The dominance of the parents was significant for the age of marriage and for the ceremony of the children's marriage. The parents arranged the marriage of their children as early as possible, usually before they were twenty years old, if economically possible. To have
grandchildren as early as possible was a sign of blessing (16, p. 27).
When no extensive education was necessary, the youth needed not delay
marriage because of it. The younger a son was married, the more domi-
nant would be the parents in the arrangement of the marriage and the
life of the son after marriage. They would also, of course, be domi-
nant in the life of the daughter-in-law.

One reason young people married early in traditional China was that
the extended family and the clan wanted to have more people, especially
sons, to perpetuate the family. In the family-oriented kinship system,
the more people an extended family had, the stronger it would become.
Therefore, the earlier the son got married, the faster the family population would grow. Also, in those periods, when machinery was not
widely used, a great deal of manpower was needed in farming and doing
household chores. All these factors contributed to early marriage of
youths.

The ceremony of the children's marriage was closely related to the
dominance of the age hierarchy in the traditional family in historical
China. Because of the high cost of the traditional marriage of the
sons, the parents were obliged to pay for it. Sometimes the parents
had to sell their property or borrow money to pay for the costs of the
big feasts in the wedding ceremony and to acquire the amount to be paid
to the bride's parents. Because the parents had paid such a big amount
of money, the son and daughter-in-law were much obliged to the parents
for their financial sacrifice (16, p. 25). The marriage ceremony was a
family affair and the family head, normally the father of the groom,
would officiate at the ritual. Neither priests nor officials were
necessary for its performance (6, pp. 38-39). The most important act
in the ceremony was to pay homage and sacrifice to the husband's ancestors, an act followed by the rite of homage to the parents of the groom.
The gathering of a large crowd of family members and kin for big feasts
also emphasized the importance of the family and kinship group. The
parents and relatives of the bride were not invited to the ceremony.
That fact signified the dominance of the groom's parents and that the
bride's parents had no authority to interfere with the life of the
newly-wedded couple (16, pp. 25-26).

Lang described the traditional marriage ceremony as follows:

For 2,500 years marriage rites adhered strictly to the forms prescribed in the ancient Book of Ritual and Ceremonies (I Li), except for some slight modifications in different regions and epochs, and the same ritual is still observed in the majority of Chinese families.

The procedure began with the matchmaker's visit to the girl's parents. If they agreed to the proposed match, they kept the gifts brought by the matchmaker and gave him a card with the girl's personal data. The eight characters standing for her name, hour, day, month, and year of birth were compared by a specialist with the corresponding data of the boy. The particulars about birth included the so-called horary and cyclical characters symbolizing animals like the rat, ox, tiger, and hare. If the girl's birth, for instance, took place on the day and hour ruled by the serpent or tiger and the boy's by the sheep or dog, the match would in inauspicious: a tiger is likely to devour a sheep or a dog. The written name may contain symbols of wood, earth, water, fire, etc. A fire symbol in the girl's name would burn the wood symbol in the boy's name; but earth or water would be favorable to wood. Later on the appearance and disposition of the prospective mates were studied as well.

This comparative analysis of the symbolic elements attached to the prospective mates was very important and can be interpreted as an attempt to insure the couple's future harmony. But as a rule, if the parents decided on the match, the symbolic elements were declared fully or "approximately" harmonious.

The next step after the exchange of cards ("the inquiry into the girl's name") was the sending of the betrothal gifts, consisting of a wild goose and a roll of silk-the equivalent of engagement ring. Very often sums of money accompanied these gifts, the amount being set after consultation with the matchmaker. The acceptance of the gifts was followed by the signing of a betrothal contract which was legally binding.

Then a fortune teller helped determine what day was propitious for the "Red Affair," the name given to a wedding because red, the color of joy and happiness, was used in the decorations. A red sedan chair was sent to the bride's home, the girl in red dress and red headgear entered it and was taken to her husband's house.

The ceremony was a family affair; neither priests nor officials were necessary for its performance. When the prescribed ritual had been observed, the marriage was legal. The family head is himself the minister of the most important Chinese religion-ancestor worship-and the head of the first administrative unit of the state. It was only natural that the state should let him perform the marriage rites (6, pp. 38-39).

The Family as the Center of Loyalty

The family was the center of loyalty in the traditional Chinese society. The family organization was structured on the principle of the Five Cardinal Relations appearing in the Book of Rites which defined and regulated the pattern of relationship of the family members, ruler-subject, and the individual in society. They are as follows: kindness on the part of the father and filial piety on the part of the son; gentleness on the part of the older brother and obedience on the part of the younger; righteousness (in its narrower sense) on the part of the husband and submission on the part of the wife; favor on the part of the senior and loyalty on the part of the subject (13, p. 51). Advocated by Confucius, the principle of the Five Cardinal Relations prescribed norms of moral conduct and established a mechanism of social control in hierarchical order of superordinate and subordinate relationships. It was a kind of informal sanction and a normative pattern for people to internalize and to live up to (13, p. 51).

The principle of the Five Cardinal Relations naturally laid strong emphasis on loyalty between members of the family and to the family as a group. In the traditional Chinese society, loyalty to the family took the first priority in a person's social obligations and was the determining factor in the total pattern of the social structure (16, p. 166). The ties of affection were the basic factor of loyalty among members of the family and were very strongly developed. They completely captured the devotion, values and attitudes of the members of a family. The family was the place of happiness, encouragement, stability, and consolation for the Chinese people (16, pp. 166-167).

The principle of Cardinal Relations defined the degree and depth of affection between family members. The strongest affection was found between parents and children, particularly between father and son, and the next strongest between husband and wife; then between brothers and sisters. Descending from the members of the nuclear family, the Chinese would treat their grandparents, uncles, aunts and cousins as closer than the members of the clan and would treat other people outside the kinship circle with some degree of distrust (16, p. 167). In order to maintain the family as the center of loyalty, an individual's social and economic interests had to come after those of the family, and compromise and sacrifice would have to be made by the individuals. Most important was that the family remained an economic structure and a unit of social interest. It required the subordination of the individuals to the interest of the group (16, p. 168). The development of loyalty in the individual members of the family began in childhood education and the children were treated as means of a primary and intimate group --the family--through personal contact and intimate interaction with other members of the family. They were taught to conform to the norms and regulations of the family and to be identified with it and proud to be a member of it (7, p. 278).

Filial piety was one of the most significant characteristics of the traditional Chinese family. In order to help the children to put filial piety into practice, a book, The Twenty-Four Examples of Filial Piety, provided models. For example, a man called Wu Mang knew that mosquitoes had bitten his parents. In order to prevent them from being bitten by more, he went up to his parents' bed and let the mosquitoes bite him. Since the mosquitoes had sucked enough blood from Wu Mang, they did not bite the parents (6, p. 25). Another man, Wang Hsiang, in order to make his parent feel comfortable, fanned his father's bed during the summer and warmed it with his body during the winter (6, p. 25).

A very inspiring example to show the filial piety of the children is the story of Kuo Chu, a poor man who had to support his wife, child, and mother. One day he said to his wife that since they were very poor and could not even support his mother, he wished to bury the child in order to support his mother. He said that they could give birth to another child, but that he could not have another mother. His wife dared not oppose him. While he was digging the grave for his son, he suddenly discovered a vase full of gold which was a reward of heaven to the filial son (6, pp. 25-26).

Another letter from Tseng Kuo-Fan illustrates his concern for his family as a center of loyalty. He was concerned for the future of his two sons, and he had his teachings and rules for the younger generations in the family.

To Chi-tseh and Chi-hung, the 13th day of the 3rd month, 1862
As I acquire more experience in life, I feel strongly how difficult it is to play the role of a teacher. You two should concentrate your efforts on your studies; you should not think of pursuing either a military or a bureaucratic career at this moment.

My teachings to the family's younger members can be summarized in what I call "eight essentials and three inducements." The study of commentaries is essential to the understanding of ancient classics; the study of phonetics is essential to the composition of poetry and prose; the pleasing of parents is essential to the performance of filial duties; the suppression of anger is essential to a healthy life; the abstinence from uttering untruthful remarks is essential to the cultivation of personal ethics; early rising is essential to the successful management of a household; incorruptibility is essential to the pursuance of an official life; and finally, friendship and harmony with the people are essential to the successful commanding of an army. The three inducements are inducements of good fortunes by observing filial piety, industriousness, and forgiveness.

My father, the honorable Chu-t'ing, emphasized one thing in his teaching: filial piety. He was respectful towards his parents when he was young, and was loving towards them when he became older. His love and respect, coming from the bottom of his heart, were genuine and sincere. When I wrote his epitaph, I emphasized one thing: filial piety... There were three kinds of people whom my grandfather, the honorable Hsing-kang, did not trust. They were Buddhist monks, Taoists, and medical doctors.

During the present time of chaos and war, the smaller the amount of money one has, the less likely he will encounter disaster. The more economical he is, the more likely he is to receive good fortune. As for you two brothers, I can see no other way whereby you can serve your mother and yourselves well except through industriousness and thrift. The military situation is extremely serious at the moment; I have only two words as my instruction: industry and thrift. Report this wish of mine to your mother and your uncles. They should not forget it either (8, pp. 352-353).

The Cult of Ancestor Worship

Ancestor worship was one of the characteristics of the traditional family in historical China and was recorded, even before 1122 B.C., among the people of Shang. Game hunting, cattle breeding and warfare were the way of life and were carried out by men. Although the status of women was low, yet the status of the deceased mother and grandmother was very high. Cattle and captured slaves were used as sacrifices and were offered to the deceased mother. Prayers were also said to her (15, pp. 8-13).

The causes of ancestor worship may be two-fold. The first is "Spiritual Immortality," which means that a man's good work, character, and virtues will be remembered by people after his death. Most likely his family members and descendants are the ones who will remember it. If a person knows that he will be remembered after his death, some of his anxiety about death may be relieved (17, p. 78). Another one is "the ghost theory" that people live as ghosts after their death and need many things. Therefore, it is necessary to have posterity to provide the needs for the deceased ancestors. Ancestral worship is at the same time ancestral remembering (17, p. 78).

Besides offering sacrifices on the graves of ancestors, the Chinese people in historical China worshipped their ancestors at home. The names of the deceased ancestors was written on a piece of tablet which was placed with other tablets. Yang has a good description of ancestor worship and its impact on the younger generation.

> There the ancestral altar in the main hall, the general dimness of the place, and the rows of golden ancestor tablets, darkened by incense smoke and reflecting the eerie light from the flickering sacrificial lamp, created a sacred atmosphere in the family dwelling, inspiring awe in the children. The constant reminder of the relationship between the living and the dead, between the existing family and the spirits of its creators, constituted a major function of ancestor worship which imposed a sense of sacredness on the family as an institution. The principles, inspired sentiments, symbols, and rituals of ancestor worship assured a religious veneration for the departed ones (16, p. 184).

The cult of ancestor worship has cultivated the attitudes of conservatism. Because posterity wanted to remember and respect deceased ancestors, it had to observe and practice what the ancestors had taught. An example could be traced to the period of Confucius as recorded in the book of Analects: "Men asked what filial piety was. The master said, it is not being disobedient." It also says, "When the father dies and for the next three years the son does not change his father's principles, he can be considered filial." (10, p. 23). Therefore, conservatism became a by-product of ancestor worship.

There are certain impacts of ancestral worship on the individuals in the traditional family. Hsu, in his Under the Ancestors' Shadow, pointed out that submission to authority and competition for a superior place in life lay the foundation of the basic personality configuration of the Chinese (4, p. 267), as, for example, when the individual shows a strong ambition toward success within the socially approved framework and for the purpose of glorifying his ancestors (4, p. 265). Also, an explicitly submissive attitude toward authority is the basic personality norm shown in overt behavior (4, p. 265). Paternal authority does not come from the living parents alone, but also from the deceased ancestors and their good behavior and virtues as well (4, p. 262).

Encouragement of Large Family

The structure of the traditional Chinese family has gone through many changes in the history of China. The Feudal Period (1100-250 B.C.) was the clan-dominated age--- social organization dominated by the clan units. The Imperial Period (from 250 B.C.-1911 A.D.) was the family-dominated age---social organization dominated by the family units. However, the Imperial Period may again be subdivided into two main eras--the Stem-family dominated Era, the period from the Ch'in (221-207 B.C.) to the Sui Dynasty (590-618 A.D.) and the Lineal-family Dominated Era, the period from the T'ang (618-906 A.D.) to the late Ch'ing Dynasty (644-1911 A.D.) (12, pp. 1-2).

It was in the beginning of the Imperial Period that the law of clan organization--patrilineal, patriarchial, father-right, sib-exogamy--was started by Duke Chou and elaborated by Confucius (551-479 B.C.) and his followers (12, pp. 1-3). After the breakdown of feudalism due to the change of method of production and distribution of goods and to the decline of the law of clan organization in the last quarter of the first millenium B.C., the government of the Ch'in Empire disrupted the extended noble families in order to weaken their opposition to the new imperial order. However, stem families of the feudal period dominated during the Han Dynasty (206 B.C.-220 A.D.). Many more nuclear family units co-existed (12, pp. 6-7). Also in the Han Dynasty, another form of clan organization evolved into "successive or esteemed clans" with a few tens of great families or lineage groups of aristocratic origin. They had special privileges in tax matters and civil service appointments, in monopolizing government offices, and in maintaining their social prestige (12, pp. 6-7).

In the beginning of the seventh century, the emperors of the T'ang Dynasty (618-906 A.D.) suppressed the "successive or esteemed clans" by abolishing many of their special privileges. At the same time, imperial decrees, laws as well as literature, encouraged extended families and opposed family divisions. Family division was not allowed when the father was still alive, except with his approval. Whenever economic strength permitted, family population would continue to grow. This type of family structure has persisted more than one thousand years among the wealthy peasants, landlords and upper classes in China up to 1949 (12, pp. 8-9).

The encouragement of the large family was an ideal in traditional China. Since it is difficult to find the structure of the family in detail in historical records, the other alternative is from semi-fiction, such as The Dream of the Red Chamber (6, p. 29) which was written during the reign of Emperor Chien Lung (1736-1795) in the Ching Dynasty (1644-1911) (11, p. 17). The author, Tsao Hsueh-chin, was born of a noble family in the Ching Dynasty, and for three successive generations the Tsaos held an important position in charge of certain affairs in

39

the royal household. The author introduced four aristocratic families --the Chias, relatives of the royal household; the Shihs, a marquis family; the Wangs, a bureaucratic family; and the Hsuehs, an imperial merchant's family and on the surface these families are prosperous and wealthy (11, p. 17).

The Chia mansion included a family of three generations, the families of several married sons and their wives and children living together in a big family (11, p. 17). It included thirty or so masters and mistresses, some of whom were aristocrats and some of whom were bureaucrats, usurers, young masters and young ladies living a comfortable life, with some 400 slaves and servants. Outside the mansion, the Chias had a number of estates which were rented to the peasants to farm who also lived on the estates. The content of the book gave lively descriptions of the complicated and complex relations among the family members (11, p. 17).

Summary and Discussion

The traditional Chinese family was structured, and has remained so, for the past two thousand years on the basis of the "law of clan organization" provided by Duke Chou and on the ethical teachings of Confucius, beginning from the fifth century B.C. The Chinese family became patrilineal, patriarchal and patrilocal. The "law of clan organization" and the ethical teachings of Confucius brought the family institution and society as well into stability and a new social order. In the traditional family, perhaps, the ideal and the actual structures coincided the closest because the family model, based on the "law of clan organization" and the ethical teachings of Confucius as an ideal, was supported and used by the rulers in traditional China to rule the country (3, pp. 19-23).

The dominance of the sex hierarchy was based on the father-son relationship in the traditional family which became a mechanism of control by the father over his children, especially sons. It was a system through which status, power and property were passed from one generation to another in the family. Man dominated in the traditional family and society, controlling all the important functions for the persistence of society, beginning from the Chou Dynasty (15, pp. 19-20). He was in control of the political, economic and educational institutions in society, and thus he was also the head of the family institution (12, p. 3). Women occupied subordinate and dependent positions in the family and society. The ideal and actual structure of the sex hierarchy in the traditional family was very closely identical because man, the ruler in the traditional society, had the power and authority and could exercise control over woman. Since woman had depended on man for her living, she was suppressed in a subordinate position which was also supported by the ideal Confucian ethics (12, p. 3).

The dominance of the age hierarchy, mainly through the patriarchal system, was used by the rulers of traditional China to rule and control the country. When the patriarch was given the responsibility and the authority to manage his family of procreation and family property, he was directly responsible to the ruler of the country for the conduct and duty of all his family members. In this case, it was a very

40

reliable method of social control and the training of good citizens. Therefore, the patriarchal system actually became the law of the country and was enforced (3, p. 22; 14, p. 360). Ideally speaking, the kinship structure based on the ethical teachings of Confucius, such as filial piety, obedience and benevolence, surely would help the rulers to control the country since good children in the family would become good citizens in society. Besides, in traditional China, adulthood and experience were essential to make a living and the older generations were important and needed to rule the family and society. Therefore, the dominance of the older generation was expected (6, pp. 11-12, 18, 56). Filial piety was used by the parents in the hope of gaining the children's support in their old age (1, p. 51). The ideal and the actual structures of the dominance of the older generation coincided very closely in the traditional family. The dominance of the patriarch in the family was a custom in traditional China as his authority had legal support (3, pp. 21-23). Filial piety became an important virtue practiced in the whole society and was supported by approval and sanctioned by defiance (16, p. 89). The parental arrangement of the children's marriage was the custom in traditional China and also, then, showed the authority of the parents and the emphasis on familism.

The family as the center of loyalty, the third characteristic of the traditional family, was the basic normative pattern and core structure of the family. Family members were given their status and taught to perform their duties. Children were taught to have filial piety towards their parents, respect towards other senior members in the family and friends. Such a socialization would extend its impact later to the larger society as those well trained and disciplined in the family would become faithful subjects to the ruler and good citizens in society. Therefore, the principle of the Five Cardinal Relations actually became the structure of kinship relations in the traditional Chinese family (16, pp. 166-168).

The cult of ancestor worship, the fourth characteristic of the traditional family, was a reinforcement of the third characteristic, the family as the center of loyalty. Ancestor worship strengthened the teachings of the deceased ancestors and respect and honor of the senior members in the family. It was a unique and significant characteristic of the traditional family and was practiced in the traditional family (16, pp. 184-185).

The encouragement of large family, the fifth characteristic of the traditional family, was perhaps a technique used by rulers and landlords in traditional China to tie the peasants down to the land. Therefore, the traditional family could contribute to a stable and orderly society in traditional China. Actually, only the wealthy families, such as the landlords and wealthy businessmen, gentry and high officials, could afford to support a large family. The most significant and reliable example and description of a large family was that of the families in The Dream of the Red Chamber in the Ch'ing Dynasty (6, p. 16).

BIBLIOGRAPHY--CHAPTER II

1. Cheng, Ch'eng-K'un, "Familism the Foundation of Chinese Social Organization", Social Forces, XXIII, No. 1, (October, 1944), 50-59.

2. "Women's Liberation - Part of the Revolution," China Reconstructs, Peking, (June, 1975), 3-6.

3. Fan, Jo-Yu, "Why We Abolished the Feudal Patriarchal System," Red Flag, V (March, 1960), 19-27.

4. Hsu, Francis L.K., Under the Ancestor's Shadow, Stanford, Stanford University Press, 1971.

5. Kam, Chai-Hsing, Social Institutions, Hong Kong, Tao Nam Publishing Co., 1966.

6. Lang, Olga, Chinese Family and Society, Archon Books, 1968.

7. Lee, Shu-Ching, "China's Traditional Family, Its Characteristics and Disintegration," American Sociological Review, XVIII (June, 1953), 272-280.

8. Li, Dun J., The Essence of Chinese Civilization, Princeton, D. Van Nostrand Co., 1967.

9. "Working Women's Struggle Against Confucianism in Chinese History," Peking Review, March 7, 1975, 17-19.

10. "Criticism of Selected Passages from 'Analects-A Confucian Classic'", Peking Review, May 9, 1975, 23.

11. "'The Dream of the Red Chamber' and Its Author", Peking Review, (May 23, 1975), 17-18.

12. Ruey, Yih-Fu, "Changing Structure of the Chinese Family," Journal of Archaeology and Anthropology, National Taiwan University, XVII, XVIII (November, 1961), 1-15.

13. Ruey, Yih-Fu, "The Five Dyads as a Means of Social Control," Journal of Sociology, National Taiwan University, III (April, 1967), 47-58.

14. Tai, Yeh-Hui, Family Law of China, Taipei, Taiwan, Cheng Wen Printing Co., 1970.

15. T'ao, Hsi-Sheng, Marriage and Kins, Taipei, Taiwan Commercial Publishing Co., 1968.

16. Yang, Ch'ing-K'un, Chinese Communist Society: The Family and the Village, Cambridge, M.I.T. Press, 1972. 5th printing.

17. Yang, Martin M.C., "Child Training and Child Behavior in Varying Family Patterns in a Changing Chinese Society," Journal of Sociology, National Taiwan University, III (April, 1967), 77-83.

CHAPTER 3

THE AGE AND SEX HIERARCHY IN THE FAMILY
IN REPUBLICAN CHINA, 1911-1949

In this chapter, the disintegration of the traditional family, attacks on the age and sex hierarchy in Republican China are examined and the forces leading to the changes are identified. It was in the Republican period that the changes in the traditional Chinese family began.

Since the family structure of Republican China does not exist any longer, the way chosen for this study was a thorough review of literature and careful selection of data. Data of this study were selected from two sources. From the U.S.A., three books, each written by a sociologist (3, 5, 9) and published by recognized university presses were used. Two American sociologists conducted studies of the Chinese family in Republican China and to obtain their data used sociological methods, such as questionnaires, interviews and participant observations (3, 5). The third book used was written by a well-known Chinese sociologist who was old enough to have lived in China at a time when he could observe those changes during the Republican period (9). A well-written article by a Chinese sociologist, published in a professional journal of sociology, and which reported the changes of the family was also used (4).

Data from Nationalist China on Taiwan included two books. One was written by a well-known sociologist and political scientist in Nationalist China (8) and he observed the disintegration of the traditional family and identified the sources of the changes. The other book was written by a well-known law professor now the President of the Judicial Yuan (cabinet) of Nationalist China (7). The latter book analyzed the Civil Code which was promulgated in 1930 and became the family law of Republican China as well as of Nationalist China. The Civil Code of 1930 has had significant impacts on the family structure, for it replaced the imperial laws based on the ethical teachings of Confucius.

Since this study has been limited to the changes on the age and sex hierarchies in Nationalist China and Communist China, with special emphasis after 1959-75, in this chapter, only the age and sex hierarchies in Republican China were examined. No conflicting evidences were found among the data as the authors observed the disintegration of the traditional family and identified the forces leading to the changes.

In the Republican Period, the traditional Confucian kinship structure was under attack and started to disintegrate after the Revolution in 1911 and the New Culture Movement in 1917. Under the influence of freedom and equality from the western culture, some intellectuals began to challenge the dominance by the older generation and by men in society and in the family.

The Age Hierarchy in the Family in
Republican China, 1911-1949

This section is divided into two parts: (1) The Traditional Kinship Structure under Attack; (2) The New Life Movement.

The Traditional Kinship Structure
under Attack

The changes in the dominance of the age hierarchy in the family in Republican China began as early as the turn of the twentieth century when the normative patterns and values of the traditional family were questioned. The introduction of the western ideas of individual liberty and rights, through direct contact with the West or through its literature, was the most potent channel of communication and influence for westernization. Youths and women began to re-examine their submissive status in the family (9, p. 16). Industrialization also played a role in causing changes. Youths left their peasant family in the country to work in the factory. They began to live in a new environment, and their family life and relations began to change. The upper and middle classes, namely the owners of modern industrial and commercial enterprises and the professional people, came to be exposed to the influence of western ideas (9, p. 17). Urbanization together with job opportunities and better living environment in the city, caused a great number of the upper and middle classes to depart from their original, traditional form of family living. The educated upper and middle classes started their own nuclear family and thus the dominance of the age hierarchy decreased (4, p. 279). The concentration of schools and colleges and newspapers in the city as well as urban occupational opportunities for women and coeducation facilitated the changes of the dominance of the age and sex hierarchy in the traditional family in the 1920's and 1930's (9, p. 17).

The Revolution and The New Culture
Movement

The success of the Republican revolution and the overthrow of the Ching Dynasty in 1911 had an important impact in the changes in the traditional family. It started the trend of destroying the guidance by Confucian ethics in the administration of the state and thus abolished the use of Confucian kinship ethics the laws to structure the traditional family (9, p. 12). The great ideological and social movement, the New Culture Movement or Renaissance of 1917, came to full force in the May 4th Movement in 1919. Family revolution was its main purpose, and it caught the attention of the public. The traditional family was the target of attack and was criticized as destructive to human rights, as suppressing the spirit of independence, and as preventing progress. The traditional dominance of both the age and sex hierarchy was under attack and the liberation of youths and the equal rights and status of women were demanded (9, pp. 12-13).

The New Culture Movement was started by young professors of Peking University, Chen Tu-Hsiu and Hu Shih and others who were the editors of the magazine The New Youth. They attacked and challenged the old system and the rule of the old men and aimed at radical changes in the social and political life in China. To achieve freedom and democracy, they argued, the Chinese youth must launch a struggle against Confucianism, which taught the absolute obedience of the children to the parents, especially to the father. The patriarchal extended family system and family loyalty were attacked as hindrances to national liberation and progress (3, pp. 109-113). Thus, although the contact of China with the West was a painful experience of foreign imperialism in the nineteenth century, the Chinese social reformers had not rejected the influence of the western thought in social movements (3, p. 113).

Further crumbling of the age hierarchy was evidenced in the mid-1920's in the Second Revolution, after Chiang Kai-Shek successfully unified China by military force after he defeated the warlords and established the national capital in Nanking in 1927 when he was a young man forty-one years old. At the same time, the Chinese Communist movement also spread in many parts of the country. Its party leader, Mao Tse-Tung, was only thirty-three. Adding further impacts to change were many young and middle aged men with modern education and important leadership positions and power in the government (9, p. 15).

The growing population mobility was another factor for the deterioration of the age hierarchy in the traditional family. By the turn of the century, China saw the growth of money economy and commercial capitalism by foreign nation's national financiers. The end result was the collapse of the agricultural economy and of handicraft. These were replaced by industry and led to the mass migration of the peasants into the city to look for employment. Because of long separation from home, the rural migrants could get away from the dominance of the older generation and the influence of the traditional family. While dominance of the patriarchal system continued in the rural area, it was rapidly deteriorating in the industrial cities (9, p. 17).

In the new dynamic society, the old men gradually lost their importance and usefulness outside the family. The accumulated experience could not cope with the fast-changing demands of skill and training in industry, professions, and even in agriculture. Industrialization gradually led to the disintegration of the self-sufficient peasant economy and thus reduced the importance and dominance of the patriarch as the leader of the family in production. Industrialization also favored the development of individualism. The requirements for efficient work and Nationalism also reduced family loyalties (3, pp. 102-103).

The New Life Movement

While changes towards westernization started in the late 1910's, an attempt to revive Confucianism was led by Generalissimo Chiang Kai-Shek and his wife between 1928-36. They tried to establish a way of life based on the mixture of Confucian rules of conduct and patterns of behavior adapted to modern capitalism (3, p. 114). The movement was launched in 1934, and the goals included revival of the ancient values of the Chinese cultural heritage and their application to conditions of modern life. Guiding virtues were propriety, justice, integrity and conscientiousness. The movement was carried to the whole country. Chiang urged use of extraordinary means to reconstruct so-

45

ciety in a New Life pattern. The birthday of Confucius was proclaimed a national holiday. Although the movement made some progress towards achieving its aims, it lost strength afterwards (2, pp. 22-23; 1, Vol. I, p. 328). Levy provides an overview of the family institution in the transitional period (5, p. 289). He observed that the kinship structure was not well-defined and was to a degree uninstitutionalized. The old patterns were dying out and the new ones were not firmly established. A great part of the old patterns continued to persist. There were some people who adopted almost completely the life patterns of the West. The great majority of the people who had been affected by new idea combined the old and the new, and very many different combinations were present. Such combinations were transitional because the two elements were incompatible for movement towards stability and institutionalization (5, p. 289).

In the eight years of war in resisting Japanese invasion (1937-1945), there was no new ideological movement affecting family reform, but the migration of millions of refugees from the coastal regions into the southwest and west of China had helped to bring changes in the traditional family there (9, p. 17). With the end of World War II in 1945 families in cities suffered the separation of family members and there was deviation still farther from the Confucian mode of the traditional family (9, p. 17).

In 1949, when the Chinese Communists took over the China Mainland, the Nationalist government moved to Taiwan. The family on Taiwan has perpetuated the traditional family structure which existed in the China Mainland before (6, p. 118).

The Sex Hierarchy in the Family in
Republican China, 1911-1949

The dominance of man over woman in the traditional family was under criticism and attack even before the establishment of the Republic in 1912. Under the influence of freedom and equality from the western culture, some intellectuals began to challenge the dominance of man in society and family. The following areas will be examined for the challenge of the sex hierarchy in the family 1911-1949: 1. The Attack on the Sex Hierarchy and the New Culture Movement, 2. The Civil Code of 1930.

The Attack on the Sex Hierarchy and
New Culture Movement

The attack on the dominance of the male sex began as early as in 1903 in the magazine Bell of the Female and in 1916 in the New Youth which criticized the patriarchal family system and the traditional marriage (8, p. 105). The western ideas of freedom and equality had stimulated the consciousness of the Chinese people, especially the intellectuals. In Bell of the Female, the editor criticized the low and subordinate status of women and the fate of women that was tied to marriage, their destiny that was dependent entirely on the husband, and her being locked up in the home. He sought the same rights for women as men had in working outside the home, in property rights, and, in the freedom of marriage and social association (8, pp. 106-107).

46

In 1916, the "Chinese Renaissance," or the "New Culture Movement," began, and it broke out in full force in the May 4th Movement in 1919. The traditional family was under attack and the term "family revolution" was used (9, pp. 12-13). Women demanded a new role in the family and in society. In the New Youth magazine, the Confucian rules of obedience (of subject to the emperor, of son to his father, of wife to her husband) were under attack as practices which made people subordinates without an independent personality (3, p. 110).

In 1925, there was another social revolution in which the feminine movement was considered part of the labor movement. Although there were the feminist movement and the principles of female liberation between 1925-1927, the feminist movement did not receive particular attention (8, p. 108). In the Second Revolution, women participated in political power. They thought that without their political participation, the emancipation could not be won. Many women became political workers in the Nationalist and Communist Parties, and some became soldiers in the Northern Expedition in 1926. In 1924, in the declaration of the first plenary session of the Nationalist Party, sex equality in law, economic matters, education and society was recognized. However, sex equality was only practiced in the cities (8, p. 108).

The Civil Code of 1930

In 1930, the Civil Code was promulgated in the China Mainland. The Code concerns kinship relations, and it is still used in Nationalist China on Taiwan today. Although sex equality is emphasized in the Code, yet the male sex is given preference in many situations. For example, both parents are legal representatives of the child, but when the parents disagree in any affairs, the father's opinion is decisive (7, pp. 294-295). Also, the father is the guardian of the children's property. But if the father cannot carry out his duty, then the mother will assume the duty (7, p. 294). After divorce, the father has the right to keep the children (7, p. 184). Although the right to be the family head can belong to both parents, the father is legally entitled to the position if there are no other methods by appointment or by election (7, pp. 357-358). However, when it comes to property rights, the wife can keep and manage her own property after her marriage, although she can pass the right of property management to her husband (7, p. 140). Daughters as well as sons have the same right to inherit family property (7, pp. 355-356). In the case of divorce, equal treatments are granted to husband and wife (7, pp. 152-153).

Summary and Discussion

The age hierarchy in Republican China was a period of transition and change. No ideal kinship structure was acceptable to the nation as a whole as the traditional Confucian kinship structure was under attack and criticism (9, pp. 12-13) and the modern, western ideal kinship structure was suggested by some intellectuals (9, p. 13).

In actuality, because there existed two ideal kinship structures in society, different kinship structures were adopted by the people. Levy observed that there were more people who kept the old with little or no change than there were those who adopted almost completely the life pattern of the West. The great majority of the people who had been affected by new ideas combined the old and the new, and all degrees of such combinations were present. Such combinations were transitional because the two were incompatible towards stability and institutionalization (5, p. 289).

The sex hierarchy in Republican China was in a transitional period as the traditional sex hierarchy was under attack and the new model of kinship relations was not yet established (5, p. 289). Because of the influence of the western ideas such as freedom and equality, the intellectuals began to attack the low and subordinate status of women and sought to provide equal opportunity of education, professional training and gainful employment of women, freedom of marriage, social association and property right. One of the solutions or achievements of the women's liberation in this period was the promulgation of the Civil Code in 1930. Ideally speaking, the Civil Code became a new family law of China.

However, the Civil Code became a compromise to the women's liberation as it reached a midpoint between the traditional and western family structures. Therefore, it gave more favorable treatment to the male than the female (3, pp. 115-116). Even with such favorable treatments to men, actually the Civil Code was not enforced because it was ahead of its time and its structure of kinship relations was not acceptable to the majority of the people. More people adhered to the traditional family structure than adopted the western pattern (5, p. 289).

BIBLIOGRAPHY--CHAPTER III

1. Boorman, Howard L., ed, Biographical Dictionary of Republican China, Vol. I-IV, New York, Columbia University Press, 1970.

2. Government Information Office, President Chiang Kai-Shek, His Life Story in Pictures, Republic of China, Taipei, Taiwan, 1972.

3. Lang, Olga, Chinese Family and Society, Archon Books, 1968. Reprint from Yale University Press, 1946.

4. Lee, Shu-Ching, "China's Traditional Family, Its Characteristics and Disintegration," American Sociological Review, XVIII (June, 1953), 272-280.

5. Levy, Marion J. Jr., The Family Revolution in Modern China, Cambridge, Harvard University Press, 1949.

6. Lung, Kwan-Hai and Shiao-Chun Chang, "A Study of the Chinese Family Organization," Journal of Sociology, No. 3, April 1967, National Taiwan University, 117-134.

7. Tai, Yen-Hui, Family Law of China, Taipei, Taiwan, Cheng Wen Printing Co., 1970.

8. T'ao, Hsi-Sheng, Marriage and Kins, Taipei, Taiwan Commercial Printing Press Co., 1968. 2nd ed.

9. Yang, Ch'ing-K'un, Chinese Communist Society: The Family and the Village, Cambridge, Massachusetts Institute of Technology, 1972. 5th Printing. Copyright 1959.

CHAPTER 4

THE WEAKENING OF THE AGE HIERARCHY IN
NATIONALIST CHINA

In this chapter, the age hierarchy in the family in Nationalist China is examined. Since the family structure in Nationalist China has been a perpetuation of the family structure of Republican China before 1949 (5, p. 118), the influence of the traditional family was anticipated. On the other hand, the Civil Code of 1930 replaced the traditional, imperial family law and is the official family law. So, a different family system was presented to the people.

Data on the family in Nationalist China included mainly three books and three articles. One book was written on the family law of China by a well-known law authority (8). Another book was written by an American sociologist and university faculty member in Taiwan who obtained his data by sociological research methods (7). Both books were published by well-established commercial presses. The third book, written by an American anthropologist, was on the family in rural Taiwan and was published by a recognized university press in the U.S.A. (10).

Three articles were included in this study and they were results of sociological studies. Two articles were results of sociological studies conducted by university faculty members of a well-known university in Taiwan and were published, in a professional journal of sociology, by a recognized university press in Taiwan (5, 9). The third article was the result of a study by two American sociologists and was published in a professional journal of sociology in the U.S.A. (6).

The studies show that there were two types of family structures on Taiwan. The studies of the peasant and working class families reported that those families still adhered to the traditional family structure while the studies on the college students' families-the educated-reported that those families followed the family pattern of the Civil Code.

Since Nationalist China has perpetuated the political and social heritage of Republican China (5, p. 118), it could be expected that the traditional teachings of the Confucian ethics would have influence in society and the family. Taiwan also was under the influence of the western culture at that time (following 1949), especially as a result of the presence of Americans. It could also be expected that the western culture could have some influence on society and the family.

In this chapter, the significant characteristics and changes of the age hierarchy in the family in Nationalist China would be examined in the following areas: 1) The Influence of the Confucian Teachings in Taiwan; 2) The Patriarchal System in a New Form; 3) The Changes in the Age Hierarchy in the Family.

The Influence of the Confucian Ethical
Teachings in Taiwan

When the Chinese Communists took over the China Mainland in 1949, the Nationalist Government moved to Taiwan in the same year. Since Taiwan was then under the rule of President Chiang Kai-Shek, it was most likely that the influence of Confucian teachings would be perpetuated. The Confucius-Mencius Society of the Republic of China was founded in 1960 for the purpose of disseminating the knowledge about the teachings of Confucius, to improve public morals, and to create a better society. Its activities include publications, monthly meetings and lectures, radio talks on the ethics of Confucius and Mencius, and guidance in the study of Confucius-Mencius teachings for student groups in the university and colleges. In 1974, it had 2198 members, mostly teachers and other professional people. Its executive council chairman, Mr. Chen Li-Fu, is a senior adviser to the President (4, pp. 322-323).

The teachings of Confucius are supported and sponsored by the national government, also, as can be seen from a speech delivered by Madame Chiang Kai-Shek to outstanding teachers in Taipei on Confucius' birthday and Teachers' Day on September 28, 1972 (3, p. 19). Madame Chiang Soong Mei-ling had been a leader of Chinese women since the 1930's and had directed the women's department in the New Life Movement in 1934. She accompanied her husband in military campaigns and served as his secretary, English interpreter, and adviser during the Second World War. She has been a good-will ambassador and personal envoy of President Chiang Kai-Shek (1, Vol. III, pp. 146-149). In her speech in 1972, she stated that the Chinese had honored Confucius for generations, that his moral heritage had influenced the Chinese culture and history for two thousand years, and that his political thought had formed a stable government. Confucius was honored as an educator and one who taught the individual, in terms of personality, for the pursuit of morality and knowledge and in terms of the family, for the cultivation of filial piety and brotherly love (3, p. 19).

The political leadership, the cultural heritage and the social environment in Taiwan has perpetuated the teachings and ethics of Confucius. In addition, with the support and encouragement of the Nationalist government, the influence of Confucian ethics has been much strengthened. The influence of Confucian ethics on the family relationship can be anticipated.

The Patriarchal System in a New Form

The patriarchal system was one of the significant characteristics of the traditional family, and the patriarch was given legal authority to manage his family of procreation and was the legal representative of his family in all legal matters. Beginning with the Civil Code of 1930, the patriarchal system has existed as a law, but in a new form. While the patriarch does not have the absolute authority and power to control and regulate his/her family members, he does, according to the Civil Code of 1930, have certain authority over the family members. His duties are to manage the family affairs, to maintain and develop the collective family life, and to protect and regulate their daily life. He is also the executor of the family regulations which will be

51

supported by law if they are not in violation of the legal code (8, p. 360). Also, he has the authority to educate and to discipline his children (8, p. 296).

In the traditional family the patriarch was the legal representative of his family of procreation and bore the legal responsibilities to pay taxes to the country and rent to the landlords. He was authorized to educate and to discipline his family members to keep the laws of the country and he would be responsible for the misconduct of his family members.

Although the head of the family does not now have to bear the legal responsibilities of the adult members, he still is responsible for the conduct of his juvenile members in the family in Nationalist China today. It is not unusual to find out that even in the 1970's the head of the family has to be responsible for the criminal actions of his family members. As recorded in the Central Daily News on May 27, 1975, the District Court of Taipei, Taiwan, made public the names of three heads of family, and it fined them from five hundred to one thousand dollars for neglecting to supervise their sons to prevent them from juvenile delinquency the second time.

The son of the first man committed an offense of physical assault on another person in 1972. The delinquent was cautioned by the Juvenile Court of the District of Taipei, and the father was warned to watch the son's behavior. Due to neglect by the family, the young man committed another offense--sexual assault on a girl between fourteen and sixteen years old. The delinquent was sentenced to go to prison for two months (2).

The son of the second man had committed a criminal offense. The delinquent was cautioned by the Juvenile Court of the District of Taipei, and the head of the family, the father, was also present. However, the legal guardian, the father, had not disciplined and supervised the young man strictly enough to maintain good conduct, and the boy committed another offense, burglary, in November 1974. The delinquent was sentenced to be placed under custody (2).

The son of the third man had committed an act of delinquency in 1973. The delinquent was cautioned by the Juvenile Court of the District of Taipei, and the head of the family was also called to be present. However, due to family head's neglect of his duty to educate and discipline, the young man committed another offense, extortion, in 1974. The delinquent was sentenced to go to prison for six months, and the imprisonment was postponed for three years by the order of the Supreme Court of Taiwan. During the period of postponement, the delinquent was placed under custody and supervision (2).

According to the judgment of the Juvenile Court of the District of Taipei, delinquents were given a hearing in the juvenile court, and some were to be placed under the supervision of the head of the family. Some were cautioned by the court in the presence of the family head. If the head of the family still did not fulfill his duty to discipline and supervise the youths so that the youths could maintain a good conduct and not commit another delinquent act, the head of the family would be punished by having to pay a fine for his negligence, and his name would be made public. Such action is based on Article Eighty-Four of the Juvenile Delinquency Code (2).

Changes in the Age Hierarchy in the Family

There are several areas to be examined on the changes in the age hierarchy in the family, such as in the family finance, marriage and education of the children. There have been a few studies on the changes in the age hierarchy in Nationalist China in the 1960's, a decade after the government moved to Taiwan. A Study of the Chinese family organization was compiled by Lung Kwan-Hai. The purpose of that study was to investigate the nature of family organization among Chinese students in Taiwan. It was based upon the return of 856 questionnaires between 1960-1964 (5, pp. 117-134). Lung's findings on the control of family finance in the university students' family of orientation in Taiwan, 1960-1964, were tabulated as follows: (5, p. 123).

TABLE I

THE CONTROL OF FAMILY FINANCE IN UNIVERSITY STUDENTS'
FAMILY OF ORIENTATION IN TAIWAN, 1960-1964

| Type of Family | Persons in Control | | | |
	Father	Mother	Both Parents	Others
Total	40.9%	29.1%	20.4%	9.6%
Nuclear	39.3	34.7	23.4	2.6
Stem	46.8	23.7	18.9	10.6
Extended	42.0	21.9	17.2	18.9
Others	23.5	38.3	14.7	23.5

Lung's finding showed deviation from the form of financial control by the patriarch in the traditional family, or by the oldest male member, or by the bread winner in the family. Lung commented that the financial situation of the family correlated with the control of financial affairs in the family. If the father could provide the family with a comfortable living, he would control the financial affairs in the family and would be respected. Otherwise, he would lose his authority and not be respected. If the family expenses were just enough or not enough, most likely the mother would control the family purse (5, p. 123). However, the oldest member of the family, namely the parent or parents, are the head or heads of the family in control of the family finance.

The second question about the age hierarchy asked was that of who made the family marriage decisions. In the traditional family, the parents arranged their children's marriage, and the purpose of marriage was to perpetuate the family lineage. However, after the founding of the Republic of 1912, the traditional legal code was abolished and has not been reestablished. According to the Civil Code of 1930, the married couple should decide by themselves on their marriage, if they are old enough (17 years for male and 15 years for female) (8, pp. 40-41).

Lung used the university students as a population in his study to find out who made family marriage decisions and what the students expected to do when they were hoping to be married. Lung's findings are shown in Table II (5, p. 124). Lung also quoted the findings from other studies to the effect that the Chinese youths prefer to select their own marriage partners, but at the same time with the approval of the parents (5, p. 124).

TABLE II

DECISION ON CHILDREN'S MARRIAGE IN UNIVERSITY
STUDENTS' FAMILY OF ORIENTATION IN TAIWAN
1960-1964

Decision of marriage given by	Percentage
Father	2.8
Mother	3.2
Both Parents	16.5
Both Parents and Children	31.1
Children	33.2
Others	13.2

Judging from the findings, only about one third of the students preferred to select their marriage partners by themselves; another one third preferred to select their own marriage partners, but with the consent of their parents; and one fifth preferred to have their marriage partners selected by their parents.

A study of attitudes of Taiwan university students towards marriage and the family was made by Marsh and O'Hara. The parental selection of a spouse, separation of sexes from puberty to marriage, absence of dating and courtship, irrelevance of romantic love, patrilocal residence, and the subordination to the husband's parents were studied. In making the comparison, six corresponding, but opposite romantic patterns of the west were used. From the findings, the hypothesis that students who say they will be able to choose their spouse themselves will favor neolocal residence was not supported. The writers explain that it is the lack of the institutional preconditions for widespread free choice of mates that accounts for the forty-two percent of the respondents in favor of the parental choice of mate (6, pp. 5-7).

O'Hara conducted a study among university students in 1971 on mate selection authority and other related questions of marriage and the family. The selected results of the study are summarized in Table III (7, p. 105). The answers to questions number two, three and six showed significant deviations from the traditional Chinese normative patterns toward the westernized pattern as the parents in the traditional family arranged the marriage of the children and the purpose of marriage was to perpetuate the family lineage. However, on question number five, about eighty-two percent of the respondents disapproved of educated women taking up full-time employment. The family and children are rated as more important than family income. The great majority of the respondents disapproved of divorce and desired stability in the marital relationship.

TABLE III

ATTITUDES OF UNIVERSITY STUDENTS IN TAIWAN
TOWARD MARRIAGE AND THE FAMILY, 1971

Questions	Answers	
	Yes	No
1. Do you want to marry?	381	1
2. Do you wish to choose your own mate?	375	7
3. Should love be the basis for marriage?	370	12
4. Is dating among university students good?	251	31
5. Is full employment for wives desirable?	65	317
6. Is a neolocal residence desirable?	309	73
7. Is the possibility of divorce dangerous to marriage stability?	345	37
8. Is the possibility of divorce harmful to your marriage?	334	48
9. Should there be an engagement before marriage?	297	35

The freedom of marriage is guaranteed by the Civil Code. The persons to be married should have free will to choose their partners and no third party should arrange and coerce a person to marry against his or her wishes (8, pp. 39-40). In actuality, many parents of the working class and peasants still arranged the marriage of their children even in the 1960's in Taiwan. A study of marriage and of family problem cases noted by the Taiwan Provincial Women's Association in Taipei, Taiwan, between 1961-1965 was conducted by the Sociology Department of the National Taiwan University. Out of 899 cases, 114 were marriage problem cases. Most of the clients (female) were between the age of twenty and twenty-five years (48 percent), and between fifteen and twenty years (25.4 percent). Only thirty percent reported their occupations. There were peasants, industrial workers, and those such as waitresses in service occupations (9, pp. 140-141).

The causes of marriage problems were many and sometimes there were more than one. The main cause was the parental interference with the daughter's marriage. It constituted 33.9 percent of all the cases. The father's interference constituted 21.3 percent, and that of the mother 12.6 percent. About one-fifth of the clients were unwilling to accept engagement which had been arranged from them by their parents or others against their own will (9, p. 142).

Several observations may be made from this information. 1) The traditional practice of parental arrangement of children's marriage still existed in Taiwan up to the 1960's, particularly among the strata of peasants and of industrial workers' families, namely, in the families of the less educated and lower strata in society. 2) The parents, particularly the father, still interfered with the marriage of their children. 3) The marriage age of the female was predominately between twenty and twenty-five years; and followed by the range from fifteen to twenty years of age. 4) There was a generational conflict between the parents and their daughters (and sons) on the matter of marriage by parental arrangement or by free choice. 5) The freedom of marriage by own choice had been wide spread and even reached the lower strata in society. 6) The courage of the daughters who dared to challenge the authority of the parents on the right of their freedom of marriage.

Still, in the rural areas, the parents have arranged most of the engagements and marriages of their children. Only a few young people selected a spouse by free choice and romantic love (10, p. 101).

The third question on the dominance of the age hierarchy was who made educational decision concerning the children? In traditional China, the head of the family decided the education and career of the children. From the same study on university students conducted by Lung, the overall result on the decision of children's education was given in Table IV (5, p. 124).

Thus, the children, by and large, could decide their own education or decide it with their parents and have thus deviated from the dominance of the age hierarchy as it was found in the traditional family. Education has, however, remained a value to the Chinese people and a channel of social mobility for the past two thousand years.

TABLE IV

DECISION OF EDUCATION IN UNIVERSITY STUDENTS'
FAMILY OF ORIENTATION IN TAIWAN, 1960-1964

Educational Decision Made By	Percentage
Father	11.2
Mother	3.2
Both Parents	18.2
Parents and Children	24.5
Children	27.4
Others	4.8

Summary and Discussion

The family structure in Nationalist China consisted of two types. One type was the traditional model, based on the traditional family system and the ethical teachings of Confucius and was practiced by the peasants and working class families--the less educated. The other type was based on the kinship relations of the Civil Code of 1930 and was practiced by the family of the college students--the well-educated. Since the Civil Code became the legal family law in Republican China and Nationalist China, it stands as the ideal family system the people should follow and adopt.

The families of orientation of college students in Nationalist China have accepted the Civil Code to a certain extent as seen from the studies in this chapter (5, pp. 117-134). However, the peasant and working class families have not accepted the Civil Code as the parents have continued to arrange the marriage of children and to decide their education and career (10). Therefore, in actuality, some of the people in Taiwan ignored the Civil Code and still adhered to the traditional practices. The Nationalist Government did not interfere with the peasant and working class families when they violated the Civil Code, until their children came to ask for legal assistance (9). It is evident that the Nationalist Government decided to leave the family affairs to the people themselves and not to force upon them the ideal family structures of the Civil Code.

BIBLIOGRAPHY--CHAPTER IV

1. Boorman, Howard L. ed, Biographical Dictionary of Republican China, Vol. I-IV, New York, Columbia University Press, 1970.

2. Taipei, Taiwan, Central Daily News, May 27, 1975.

3. China Yearbook, 1972-73, Taipei: China Publishing Co., 1973.

4. China Yearbook, 1975, Taipei: China Publishing Co., 1975.

5. Lung, Kwan-Hai and Shiao-Chun Chang, "A Study of the Chinese Family Organization," Journal of Sociology, No. 3, April 1967, National Taiwan University, 117-134.

6. Marsh, Robert and Albert R. O'Hara, "Attitudes of University Students Towards Marriage and the Family in Taiwan," American Journal of Sociology, (July, 1961) 1-8.

7. O'Hara, Albert R., Social Problems: Focus on Taiwan, Taipei, Taiwan, Mei Ya Publications, Inc., 1973.

8. Tai, Yen-Hui, Family Law of China, Taipei, Taiwan, Cheng Wen Printing Co., 1970.

9. Ting, Polly P.Y. Chi and Mei-Lein Huang, "The Statistical Analysis of Marriage and Family Problem Cases of Taiwan Provincial Women's Association," Journal of Sociology, National Taiwan University, Taipei, April 1967, 137-152.

10. Wolf, Margery, Women and the Family in Rural Taiwan, Stanford, Stanford University Press, 1972.

CHAPTER 5

THE AGE HIERARCHY BEING CHALLENGED
IN COMMUNIST CHINA

In this chapter, the age hierarchy in Communist China is examined. For the past two thousand years, there existed the dominance of the age hierarchy in the family in traditional China, namely, the dominance of the older generation over the younger generations. When the Chinese Communists took over the China Mainland in 1949, they have tried to eliminate the dominance of the age hierarchy in the family.

In this chapter, the ideal structure of the family as established by the Communists is identified and examined as is the actual structure of the family showing how the people responded to the indoctrination and demands of the Communists. As Communist China is a totalitarian state and not an open society, it has been impossible for social scientists to go in to conduct sociological studies. Therefore, an indirect method was chosen for this study through using a thorough review of literature and careful selection of data. The data were divided into two types, namely the data of the ideal family structure and of the actual family structure.

The data on the ideal structure of the family were collected through the review of literature from the articles published by official organs of the Communist Government as only the official organs could publish such directives and policies for the people to follow. Therefore, nine articles on the ideal family structure on the age hierarchy published by five periodicals (1, 3-7, 10, 17) and one newspaper (15) were included as they were official organs of the Communist Government.

The data on the actual family structure included two articles published in Communist China, two articles and one book published in the U.S.A. and an interview of an informant by the present writer. In Communist China, the Communist occasionally published the criticisms and complaints of the people on the Communist policies, and opinion opposite to the Communist ideology were allowed to be published in the newspapers and periodicals. Therefore, two articles from the Communist periodicals were included (3, 7).

The data on the actual family structure from the U.S.A. included two articles written by two American sociologists on the family in Communist China and published in two professional journals (9, 12). Also selected was a book written by a Chinese sociologist on the family in Communist China and published by a recognized university press (16). The three writers obtained their data through the review of literature and interviews with Chinese refugees who had left the China Mainland. Lastly, the present writer interviewed a close relative who visited Communist China in December 1975 (8).

There were conflicting evidences on the data collected between the ideal and the actual family structures in the age hierarchy. The Communists proclaimed their ideal family structures for the purpose to weaken the dominance of the age hierarchy but in actuality the dominance of the head of the family in education, work and marriage of the children still existed, especially in rural areas.

The aims of the Communists to challenge the age hierarchy are clear. As Communist China is a totalitarian state, it demands the absolute and sole loyalty of its people to the state and the party. Therefore the Communist government would try its best to suppress or eliminate any social institutions or agencies which would compete for the loyalty of its people, especially for the younger generation, the young people and children.

The traditional Chinese family was the center of loyalty for the Chinese people. The sustaining structure of the traditional family was the relationship between the parents and the children, particularly the children's filial piety towards the parents. Therefore, the Communists have aimed to weaken or eliminate that social structure in the family (which was the strength of the traditional family). The Communists have launched ideological attacks and indoctrinations and have tried to change the thinking of the people even in the early 1950's. The new Marriage Law was promulgated on May 1, 1950 and the following few years might be called the period of the new Marriage Law movement. In 1958, the people's commune was established and the nationalization of industry and commerce was also completed. The attack on the age and sex hierarchy in the family began in the 1960's and have continued to the 1970's. In this chapter, the challenge on the age hierarchy in Communist China was examined as follows: 1) The Attack on the Patriarchal System and Filial Piety, (2) Change in the Decision on Education and Career of Children, 3) Changes on the Decision of Children's Marriage.

The Attack on the Patriarchal System and Filial Piety

If the age hierarchy in the family was to be broken down, the patriarchal system had to be abolished first. Therefore, the attack on the traditional patriarchal system was launched on the ideological front. A special article was written by Fan Jo-Yu of Communist China in 1960 to explain why the patriarchal system was abolished. Fan, later an associate editor of the Red Flag (Hung Ch'i) magazine from 1964-1967 (13, p. 203), stated that since the Communists took over the China Mainland in 1949, the social structure and functions of the family have been weakened and changed. With the abolition of the private ownership of the means of production and the establishment of the people's communes, the rural family, ideally speaking, was no longer a basic unit of production or entirely an economic unit for consumption. The commune operated dining halls, nurseries, and sewing teams, and the socialization of family labor could be carried out. Many of the peasants' lives were no longer involved with the family, and that fact made the family not entirely a unit of consumption. The patriarch was no longer in control of the means of production. Further, the family was no longer in charge of the function of socialization. That function was taken over by the government, and the function of discipline and punishment were also taken over by the legal institution (6, p. 26). The authority of the patriarch to arrange for the marriage of his children and to decide the education and career of the youths was also challenged and abolished.

When the traditional patriarchal system was abolished, however, there still would be a person who would be the head of the family. That person may be a man or a woman, someone from the older generation or from the younger generation, but would be the most politically and ideologically advanced person and would be respected in the family (6, p. 27).

In this new type of family, the problems would be due to contradictions between the comparatively advanced and the backward members in the family. These contradictions could be solved by a desire for unity and through criticism and self-criticisms. It could achieve unity based on a new foundation without the need for any family regulations. In this new type of family based upon democratic unity, the family relations would be that "father and son respect one another, husband and wife live in harmony and brothers are friends" (6, p. 27).

Changes such as the above make it clear that the Communists have sought to destroy the traditional patriarchal system which had dominated the Chinese people for the past two thousand years. With the destruction of the patriarchal system, the people can be set free from the familial dominance, and the Communist government will then have eliminated a rival for the control of its people. Such an ideological indoctrination naturally would initiate contradiction in the family, since the ideologically advanced family members, usually the younger generation, would challenge the older generation in the leadership in the family when the latter could not tolerate the former's behaviors that deviate from the traditional normative patterns. With economic independence and the support of the Communists, the younger generation could shake off the dominance of the patriarch, in urban areas in particular.

Besides the formal and informal control of the patriarch, supported by laws or customs, the integrity of the Chinese family, even in its modern form, also depends on emotional ties between its family members. The parents love their children and build up strong emotional ties among them. In return, the children develop filial piety towards their parents (2, p. 51). The Communists eliminated the authority of the patriarch functionally by the abolition of the functions the traditional family had performed--those of production and consumption, socialization, and legal, formal and informal social controls. However, a study conducted through interviews of the Chinese refugees in Hong Kong showed that in the rural area, the father is still the head of the family by custom and the family is still an economic unit and has the authority to decide on the education and career of the youths (12, p. 715).

In their attack on filial piety, the Communists also relied heavily on ideological weapons. The Communists believe that the relations between father and son must be viewed from the foundation of social relations. They may be the relations of comrades if both of them are party members; between a party member or youth league member on the one hand, and the masses of the working people on the other. They even may be the relations of enemies if one of them is a landlord, counterrevolutionary or bad element (17, p. 93). Whether a son should obey his father or not will depend on what the father says. If his teachings are for the revolution, the son will obey him; if not, the son can reject them. This clearly is a deviation from the traditional norm that the son should obey his father's order without question (17, p. 94). Relations are determined, not by the kinship system, but by the classes the people belong to. The basic interest is to safeguard the class interests of the proletariat and whole-heartedly serve the people. Therefore, they put the revolutionary interests above every- thing else. If bad things were to be done by the enemy to damage the interest of the proletariat, one should launch resolute struggles. If done by those among the people themselves, one should do ideological work or make serious criticism (17, p. 94). Always safeguarding of the interests of the proletariat is above the interests of the family.

The Communists state that the filial piety of the laboring people is different from the feudalistic filial piety. In the former, the respect of the aged and the support of the aged parents are viewed as the duty which the children should fulfill and are built upon the good character of mutual love. These two types of filial piety must be dis- tinguished (5, p. 17). The Communists still honor filial piety and respect of the senior if the interests and benefits of the state are placed in priority.

Another attack is on the support of the aged parents. Whereas, in traditional China, support of the aged was urged on the basis of filial piety, the Communists see the support of the aged parents from a dif- ferent viewpoint. In a socialist society, the children's support of the aged parents is based upon the general principle of serving the people. When a person is able to produce in society, he participates in the production of material wealth and contributes his labor to so- ciety. When a person loses his capability of production, he will be supported and taken care of by society. The care and support of the aged is a social obligation (17, p. 96).

The problems of parental love, filial piety and the support of the aged parents were dealt with by the Communists in their answers to the letters written by the youths who were puzzled by these problems. A letter purportedly written by a young worker called Shan Kuang, in Canton, in 1965, was answered as follows:

Comrade Editor:
I am a young worker from a landlord family. Since leaving school not long ago, I have been at my present work post. Under party education, I have set my heart and mind on doing a good job of my work so I can step up my thought reform and strive for progress.
Recently, however, I received a number of letters from my parents, saying: "Now that you are working, you can earn money. But don't forget to return gratitude to your parents. You should know we have fed you and brought you up!"
I have wavered somewhat. I am their only son. In the past they always regarded me as "the darling of the family."
I think a person, after all, is brought up by par-

ents. Parental love for their children stems from "natural" feelings. So long as children draw a clear line of
class distinction with their parents politically, it is a
customary human feeling for the former to maintain feeling
of kinship with the latter.

It is indeed obligatory for children to be grateful
to their parents for their upbringing. However, some comrades disapprove of my view. How should I view and handle
this kind of family feeling, comrade editor? I hope you
will help me raise my level of understanding. (Signed)
Shan Kuang (15).

Shan Kuang:
Comrade editor of Study and Life has passed your letter to me. After reading it, I think the question you have
brought up is essentially one of whether or not we should
use the class viewpoint to look at the problem of "family
feeling."

When young people from families of the exploiting
classes think of ways of drawing a clear line of class distinction with their families, they often will come upon the
problems of so-called "feelings of kinship" and "the need
for returning gratitude to one's parents."

If we do not look at these problems from the class
viewpoint, it will be impossible to draw a clear distinction
with families of the exploiting classes. Nor can we firmly adhere to the proletarian stand.

You have said you parents have regarded you as the
"darling of the family." This is what you think is love,
isn't it? As a matter of fact, in the world there is no
such a thing as love for no reason at all.

In a class society, love always has class character.
Abstract love is nonexistent. In saying that parents of
the exploiting classes have love for their children, the
motivation for "love" in this class lies in the fact that
they want to pin their hopes on their children and posterity so that they will maintain and carry on the interests of the exploiting classes and become their successors.
Here, there is absolutely no supraclass, "natural" love to
speak of.

In the past, your parents obtained by means of exploitation from working people all the food they ate,
clothes they wore, things they used, and the house they
lived in. After liberation, you were also indebted to the
Party and working people for providing you with the means
whereby you were able to attend school.

Therefore, as far as those from families of the exploiting classes are concerned, it is working people--and
not your parents of the exploiting classes--who truly have
brought you up.

If you want to be grateful for your upbringing, then
you should return gratitude to the laboring people. Cer-
tainly you should not return gratitude to your parents of
the exploiting classes .. (15).

The Communists thus have tried to interpret the children's love
r their parents from a class viewpoint and eventually tried to di-

vide the children and their parents into two class lines, the bourgeoise and the proletariat, the two being always in an antagonistic and conflicting relationship.

However, there appeared to have developed a severe social problem centered on the support of the aged parents in the 1950's. The December issue (1956) of Chinese Youth magazine was especially dedicated to the problem of the support of the age parents. The editor received a large number of letters from the readers revealing that they had not supported their parents and had not respected or cared for other aged persons. They understood their mistakes and were sorry for their neglect. They also uncovered how their neighbors and friends had discriminated against, mistreated, or abandoned their parents (3, p. 29), most likely in urban areas.

The editor tried to strongly warn the public about this severe social problem and to correct it as soon as possible. He emphasized that the family had a close connection with life in society. A family relationship of mutual love would create an orderly and good life in society. A harmonious family life among its members was an expression of the spirit of mutual love and care; and a happy family life could be a reflection of the warmth of the new society. He warned that family relations, ethics and morality were parts of the superstructure which had to be changed when the infrastructure, namely, the economic institution, was changed. When the Communists tried to change the traditional filial piety which put the interests of the family above those of the people and the country, the people were warned that they should not imitate the bourgeoisie who abandoned their parents and children because they had built their family relations on the basis of money (3, p. 29).

While the Communists were in the process of abolishing the traditional kinship system and its practices, however, one must recognize the invaluable virtues and morality of the laboring people perpetuated for several thousand years, such as that "the aged, widowed, orphans, disabled would be taken care of" and "to care for the aged as I care for my aged parents and to care for others' children as my own children." Such virtues had to be perpetuated in the new society. One must distinguish between the feudalistic ethics and morality with the virtues of the laboring people. If the virtues of the laboring people were abolished, it would be very difficult to build up the new ethical relations. Therefore, those youths who had mistreated and abandoned the parents must be severely warned and educated. All the youths in China must pay close attention to the problems that they should be educated to care for their parents and respect their seniors (3, p. 29).

In order to bring the family back to integrity and harmony, the editor of the Chinese Youth magazine included another essay, that one entitled "Establish the Honorable Ethical Relationship of Communism." Having accused those youths who were contaminated with the extreme individualism of the bourgeoisie and who had abandoned their parents, he further elaborated that if the retired and aged parents were abandoned by their children, that would put the duty of the support for the aged upon society and the state and that would be detrimental to the construction of socialism and create severe social problems (4, p. 14). Besides, it was against the law to do so because "the children have the duty to support and assist their parents," as recorded in Article

64

Thirteen, Chapter Four, of the Marriage Law of the People's Republic of China, promulgated on May 1, 1950 (4, p. 14).

The editor even suggested that the young married couples should ask their parents to live with them. Even though in the future when old age homes would exist for the aged, it would be a good thing for the aged parents to live with a son or a daughter on long term or temporary basis because of the love between them. The relations between parents and children should consist both of feelings and responsibility. Although the children should not give in to the interference of the parents on important issues, the children should tolerate their parents on unimportant matters, such as their religious beliefs, if they could not persuade the parents to change. Therefore, the relationship between parents and children should be based on principles and facts, upon traditions as well as new situations, and upon the daily life as well as feelings (4, p. 14).

Several possibilities seem to exist in light of the above articles. Having blamed the bourgeoisie for contaminating the thought of some young people, the Communists had to modify some of their ideological interpretations. Actually, it was their attack on the age hierarchy which created an anomaly, a very confused and ambivalent situation. Most of the Chinese people have not abandoned their aged parents even when they live in a capitalistic society anywhere.

It might be that when the Communists elevated the status of the young conflicts between the older generations and the youths were unavoidable. After the confrontation in many issues, the aged lost their battle, as they had no economic and legal power such as they had had before. Without the support and link of the filial piety of their children, the aged parents might be treated as strangers or even enemies in the family.

The third cause of conflict might be the hardship in life in Communist China. The salary a person made might barely be enough to support himself and his family, and there were deficiencies meeting many basic daily needs.

Consequently, the Communists had to slow down on their attack on the age hierarchy when the situation had gotten out of hand. After all, they had to establish a new normative pattern and ethical relations for the people to follow.

Changes in the Decisions on the Education and Career of Children

Since the Communists took over the China Mainland in 1949, the decisions on the education and career of the children have not been entirely controlled by the parents, particularly not by the patriarch. The political ideology of Communism, the political cadres and party education had also considerable influence on education and career decision of the youths (7, pp. 24-26). However, after the Cultural Revolution in 1967, admission into the university, which has been a value by itself, came to be completely handled by the Party. Only youths with working experience, good family background, political thinking, and performance will be selected to be students in the university.

After their university education, they will return to the positions where they have come from and continued their services (11, pp. 13-15).

Before the Cultural Revolution, the Communists had tried very hard to change the ideas of education and career from the traditional Chinese conception, and the youths were chosen as targets for indoctrination. Based on the traditional concept of education, Mencius taught that "those who work with their minds govern, those who work with their hands are governed." Other popular proverbs were "Studying surpasses everything" and "Studying well is to become an official." The characteristics of the traditional concept of education are that mental labor is superior to manual labor; the purpose of education is to enter the civil service from which a person would be rewarded with wealth, status, prestige and power. (More detailed discussions of these are to be found in chapter eight.)

The Communists indoctrinated the youths with different ideas by saying that the purpose of education is not for self interests but to serve others. Also, a person should not look down on manual labor; and on the contrary, one should identify and unite with the working class, namely the proletariat. Therefore, a large number of educated youths have been sent to the countryside to work as peasants (10, pp. 19-21).

Since the Communists have taught a different conception of education and career, there are bound to be conflicts between the parents and the children on the decision of education and career of the latter. With the aid of the Communists, the youths dared to challenge their parents on the authority and decisions of education and career. The Communists always like to use a model hero to educate the people. A very inspiring model for them is Fang Yu, the daughter of a university professor in Nanking.

Fang Yu's family had an intellectual tradition, and education was highly valued. Therefore, the parents and the grandmother put their hopes on Fang Yu and her younger brother to become scholars and intellectuals in the future, especially to become scientists and give glory to the family. Her grandmother was proud of the prestige of her son and the material enjoyments they had as the family of five lived in a house of seven rooms, supplied by the government. The following account is from Chinese Youth (7, pp. 24-26).

Yu was encouraged to devote full time to her studies and discouraged from doing any house chores and manual labor. Having received the class and labor education for the past few years, she gradually realized what was right or wrong judged from the Communist doctrines. She then realized that her father and family had used knowledge as a channel of social mobility to get their personal prestige, status and material needs, and she also realized how selfish and cunning they were. She decided not to follow the path of the capitalist intellectuals. On the contrary, she would follow the path of the Communists directed by the Party.

In the final year in the high school, Yu once again thought about her future career according to the needs of the Party. She realized that she had been deeply influenced by the thinking of the bourgeoisie, and that therefore it would be good for her to go among the laboring people and to live a hard life to transform into being a proletarian. At that time, educated youths were badly needed in the countryside. Although life was difficult in the rural areas, for the need of revolutionary construction she decided to break the bondage of the family and participate in the agricultural front.

When Yu told her family that she decided not to take the admission examination into the university, but rather had decided to go to the countryside to become a peasant, her parents and grandmother were shocked and said that she was completely mixed up and cautioned her not to fall into the trap of the wicked people. She was told to come home every Sunday from school. Her father tried to use the Communist policy to trick her as he said that she had not obeyed the Party to have "one heart to make two preparations" (to take the entrance examination and to be prepared to go to the countryside) and to be selected by the Party. He also said that the contributions of a scientist would be much bigger than those of a peasant, and that a scientist's name would be remembered for a long time, and that she had no ambition or high ideal. However, she replied that a person's ambition, ideal, and dedication depended on whether or not a person was willing to serve the people and was not to be judged by the kind of work done; ambitions had class character.

She decided to be the successor of the revolution and to build up the countryside of socialism. Her father continued to try to persuade her and asked if she was not sorry to do this, since she was well-qualified to go to the university. Also, he ridiculed her by saying that she was afraid to take the university entrance examination. He finally warned her that if she did not take the entrance examination, he would no longer recognize her as his daughter. She replied that it did not matter if she was his daughter or not; what really mattered was that she was the daughter of the Communist Party.

Then came her mother and grandmother to do the persuading. Her grandmother tried to entice her with the material comforts their family had and scolded her that she had no ambition and asked for hardships which she did not deserve. She then told Yu the hardships in the countryside--that there was not enough to eat and wear and that one had to work very hard in the field, and that nine out of ten youths who had been sent to the countryside could not stand the hardship and had to ask for money, food, etc., from home. The grandmother further threatened her that no material goods would be sent to her in the countryside, and finally she knelt down before her granddaughter and begged her to change her mind. But when her granddaughter refused to do so, she beat her.

The struggle with her family lasted about a year. Of course, Yu struggled within herself. She had to face the temptation to pursue further study in the university and academic success and at the same time the callings of the revolution were ringing in her ears. She was expected to be a revolutionary to serve the laboring people with her knowledge and culture which she could be tempted to use as a channel of social mobility for her selfish interests. Being a member of the Communist Youth League, she decided to pay back and serve the laboring people who had supported her education. Then she imagined that she could be ridiculed by her family and neighbors but she stood firm on her decisions to be a revolutionary youth and dare to rebel against the forces of tradition. She realized she was involved in critical class struggle and that she must be on high alert. She then realized that it was the Party organization, teachers, classmates, the writings of Chairman Mao and the brilliant influences of heroes that had created a dynamic force to support her. In the year-long struggle with her family, the principal, the committee secretary of the Youth League and the teacher of her class talked with her many times and helped her to see the direction of progress. The Youth League had encouraged her several times and thus strengthened her faith in victory. Finally, she was in the countryside but the ideological struggles were still in her mind on the dilemma of being a peasant or going to the university. At the same time, her father had no change in his attitude and still ridiculed his daughter for choosing a wrong and degrading direction. He then turned his attention to his son and to try to make him go to the university.

One can see, then, the tactics the Communists used to carry out their revolution on the family. Through the education in Communist ideology, group relationships such as the Youth League and the association of Party members and cadres, they seek to win the youths to their side. Of course, their success will depend on the acceptance of their doctrines by the youths. To help secure that they used emotional supports and the great calling of the proletarian revolution to attract the youths to shift from one class position to another, to firmly stand alongside the proletariat, and to serve the great majority with one's whole being.

Since most of the intellectual youths came from the families of the upper middle and upper classes and educated stratum before the Cultural Revolution in 1967, where the traditional Confucian ethics gained strong support, the patriarch was more willing to support the education and career for the younger generation. However, the patriarch's authority and influence on the education and career of the youths have been challenged by the Communists and the youths could decide themselves. Anyhow, there are only two choices--to follow the proletariat to serve the people or to follow the bourgeoisie to pursue individualistic self-interests.

In their revolution against the family, the Communists relied heavily on the educational and associational approaches rather than force. They rather saw the youths to have a complete ideological reform themselves and even suffered persecutions to test their determination. The Communists want their followers to accept the orders of the Party willingly, unconditionally and without question. Fang Yu's determination, struggle, sufferings and courage surely had won much more compassion, support and positive results than in the case where Communists stepped in to suppress the parents and the grandmother. So, they let Fang Yu fight the whole battle from the beginning to the end without outside interference. She had successfully rebelled against her family in deciding upon her education and career, and she was thus, viewed as a heroine in the nation.

However, after the Cultural Revolution in 1967, the education and career of the youths have been controlled by the local Communist government. According to the report of an informant who is a very close relative of the present writer and visited the China Mainland in December 1975, all the high school graduates in the cities have been sent to the different parts of the country away from home. According to the allocation by the local government, these youths worked in different occupations and quite many of them were assigned to work in the farm. At least after two years of work, some of the youths would be selected and recommended by their working units to pursue further studies in the university if their family background is good (from the working class), their political consciousness is high, and if there are political activities (8).

So, it is evident that the head of the family has lost authority to control the education and career of the children in the People's Republic of China after the Cultural Revolution.

Decision on Children's Marriage

In the traditional Chinese family, the parents, especially the father, were responsible for the decision about marriage of their children. However, when the Communists took over the China Mainland in 1949, a new Marriage Law was promulgated by the Central People's Government on May 1, 1950. In the new Marriage Law, the Communists were openly against the marriage by arrangement and interference by the third party as recorded in Chapter I of the Marriage Law.

ARTICLE 1
The feudal marriage system based on arbitrary and compulsory arrangements and the supremacy of man over woman, and in disregard of the interests of the children, is abolished.
The New-Democratic marriage system, which is based on the free choice of partners, on monogamy, on equal rights for both sexes, and on the protection of the lawful interests of women and children, is put into effect.

ARTICLE 3
Marriage is based upon the complete willingness of the two parties. Neither party shall use compulsion and no third party is allowed to interefere.

ARTICLE 6
In order to contract a marriage, both the man and the woman should register in person with the people's government of the district or township in which they reside. If the proposed marriage is found to be in conformity with the provisions of this Law, the local people's government should, without delay, issue marriage certificates.
If the proposed marriage is not found to be in conformity with the provisions of this Law, registration should not be granted.

Under the new Marriage Law, the parents would not arrange or interfere with the marriage of their children. Besides, both the man and the woman would register in person with the people's government of the district and they would be examined by the government to see if their marriage were based on free choice and was in compliance with the Marriage Law. If so, a marriage certificate would be granted. The issuance of a marriage certificate is new to the traditional family as marriage in traditional China was considered as a family business and was handled by the head of the family (16, p. 26).

Although the Marriage Law was promulgated in 1950 and although the Communists tried to use all efforts to put it into practice (16, p. 208), it is estimated that its effectiveness could only reach fifteen percent of the population living in the cities and towns (14, p. 140). The vast majority of the rural population still ignored its existence and the old practice of marriage by purchase still existed in the 1950's (16, pp. 210-211). An American sociologist interviewed the Chinese refugees in Hong Kong who had left Communist China in the past two decades and discovered that marriage by free choice was practiced mostly among urban youths of professional and white-collar occupations (12, p. 708). Another type of marriage was that the future spouses were introduced and fiances got to know each other before marriage. Inactive village youths, who were shy and those in professions which are exclusively male, had difficulty in finding suitable mates and had to rely on friends and relatives to introduce them to prospective mates (12, p. 710). A third type of marriage, adopted by the majority of youths in the rural areas, was a marriage arranged mostly by parents with the consent of the future spouses. No effort was made to build up a relationship before marriage (12, p. 711). A fourth type of marriage was the arranged marriage in which the future spouses had never met before their marriage. Only five percent of the respondents married after 1949 belonged to this category (12, p. 711).

Summary and Discussion

When the Communists started to attack the age hierarchy in the early 1960's, they believed that actually a new type of family structure based on the Communist ideology would emerge after the establishment of the communes in 1958. Mess halls, nursery were built in large numbers and socialization of household chores was planned (6, p. 26). However, after the trial for a few years, the large scale commune type of family life failed and collapsed (9, pp. 629-630) and once again the family is still a unit of consumption and partial unit of production (9, pp. 616-625). Because of the relationship of production, the relationship in the family is still strong as the family members have to depend on one another, in rural areas in particular (9, pp. 616-621).

As the patriarchal system was abolished in Communist China and the youths could gain independence by making a living by themselves outside the family, especially the city youths, they can challenge the authority of the older generation in their family of orientation with the support and assistance of the Communists. For example, university students were encouraged by the Communists to reveal and criticize the past history of their parents and other family members in the Five-Anti and the Three Anti movements (16, pp. 101, 176-180). More recently, in the Cultural Revolution in 1966, the present writer was told in 1971 that one of his young relatives, being a Red Guard in Canton, destroyed and burned all the ancestors' tablets in the family as a part of the revolution against the "old" culture. Since the Red Guard had the encouragement and support of the local Communists, the older family members could not stop her from burning the ancestors' tablets. Such an act was a very serious "crime" in traditional China because such an act was a big insult to one's ancestors and family lineage. That person is an infidel and criminal in the family and such an act must be stopped in the traditional family. The ancestors' tablets were taboo symbols in the family and were reverently protected and honored because they represented the spiritual residence and presence of the deceased ancestors. The present writer remembered in his youth that ancestors' tablets could not be touched, a restraint indicating them to be highly honored at home.

In Communist China, the head of the family, especially in urban areas, has lost his absolute power and authority to control the education (higher education) and work allocation of his children, when compared with the patriarch in the traditional family. Ideally speaking, the Communists have tried to educate and indoctrinate the youths to accept the work allocation and education opportunities by the local government willingly (7, pp. 24-26); but in actuality many of the urban youths were not satisfied with their work allocation and education opportunities and left their work allocations. (This is discussed in more detail in chapter ten).

In Communist China the decision about the children's marriage was officially taken away from the head of the family, namely the parent or parents, by the Communists. Ideally the Communists believed and have tried to destroy the parental arrangement of children's marriage (1), but actually the parents still have had considerable influence on the children's marriage, especially in rural areas (12, pp. 705-717).

If a general conclusion is needed to describe the age hierarchy and kinship relations between the parents and children in Communist China today, it would be that the relationship between the parents and the children is in a reverse proportion to the children's participation and performance in the political activities, if the older generations are not political activists. In other words, the more actively the younger generation participates and performs in political activities, the weaker the relationship in the family between the parents and the children. Conversely, the less active the children are involved in political activities, the stronger their relationship would be with their family. The reason is that many of the political activities in Communist China have been in contradiction with the traditional family structure. Besides, the more time a person spends outside his family in political activities, the less time he will have to be with his family members.

BIBLIOGRAPHY--CHAPTER V

1. Central People's Government of the People's Republic of China, The Marriage Law of the People's Republic of China, promulgated on May 1, 1950, Peking.

2. Cheng, Ch'eng-K'un, "Familism the Foundation of Chinese Social Organization," Social Forces, XXIII, No. 1, (October, 1944), 50-59.

3. "Should Not Mistreat and Abandon Your Parents" editorial, Chinese Youth, (December 1, 1956), 29.

4. "Establish the Honorable Ethical Relationship of Communism," Chinese Youth, (December 16, 1956), 14.

5. Chu, Pak-Kun, "On Filial Piety," Chinese Youth, (December 16, 1956), 17.

6. Fan, Jo-Yu, "Why We Abolished the Feudal Patriarchal System," Red Flag, Hung Ch'i, (March 1, 1960), 19-27.

7. Fang, Yu, "Breaking the Family Bondage and Becoming a Good Child of the Proletariat," Chinese Youth, (November 1, 1964), 24-26.

8. Interview with a potential informant in January 1976.

9. Parish, William L. Jr., "Socialism and the Chinese Peasant Family," Journal of Asian Studies, Vol. XXXIV, No. 3, May 1975, 613-630.

10. "Taking the Revolutionary Path of Going to the Countryside," Peking Review, May 10, 1974, 19-21, 31.

11. "Peasant-College-Peasant," Peking Review, (February 14, 1975), 13-15.

12. Salaff, Janet W., "The Emerging Conjugal Relationship in the People's Republic of China," Journal of Marriage and the Family, (November, 1973), 705-717.

13. Union Research Institute, Who's Who in Communist China, Vol. I, Hong Kong, Union Press, 1969.

14. Walker, Richard L., China Under Communism, New Haven, Yale University Press, 1955, in Lucy Jen Huang "Some Changing Patterns in Communist Chinese Family," p. 140, Marriage and Family Living (May, 1961), 137-146.

15. Canton, Yang-Ch'eng Evening News, Yang Ch'eng Wan Pao, April 6, 1965.

16. Yang, Ch'ing-K'un, Chinese Communist Society: The Family and the Village, Cambridge, Massachusetts Institute of Technology, 1972, 5th Printing. Copyright 1959.

17. Yen, Chang-Kuei, "We Must Resolutely Discard Feudal Morality," _Philosophical Research_, Che-hsueh Yen-chiu, (November 25, 1963) 93-101, NTIS.

CHAPTER 6

THE WEAKENING OF THE SEX HIERARCHY IN
NATIONALIST CHINA

In this chapter, the sex hierarchy in the family in Nationalist China--the dominance of men over women in the same generation and below--was examined. Ideally, the equality between the sexes is guaranteed, written in official and legal documents, by the Nationalist Government. Such ideals have not been enforced, however, by the government which has left the acceptance of those ideals and law to the people themselves. Therefore, discrepancies between the ideal and actual structures have been observed.

Data collected for this chapter mainly came from publications in Taiwan. The data on the ideals of sex equality were collected from public documents which were published by official organs of the Nationalist Government and therefore could express the official opinions (1, 2). Besides, a book on the family law of China written by a law authority and published by a well-established commercial press was included as it could interpret the Civil Code on the kinship relations in Nationalist China (7).

Data on the actual structure of sex hierarchy in the family in Nationalist China were collected from two books, two articles and official documents as well. A book written by a university faculty member in Taiwan and was published by a well-established commercial press (6). Another book was written by an American anthropologist on her study on the women and the family in rural Taiwan and was published by a recognized university press in the U.S.A. (10). An article was the study on the marriage and family problem cases by university faculty members in Taiwan and was published in a professional journal of sociology there (9). Another article was written by an American anthropologist on the women of Taiwan and was published in a professional journal of Chinese studies in the U.S.A. (3). Demographic statistics on the education and employment of the female were collected from official documents published by the Nationalist Government as they were the only source available (4, 5, 8).

There were conflicting evidences on the data collected. Discrepancies between the ideal and actual structures in sex equality were observed. The discrepancies and deviations were greater among the peasant and working class families.

In Nationalist China, sex equality has been the ideal structure in society and the family and has been expressed and guaranteed by the Nationalist Government (2, p. 446). Besides, the western culture has continued to influence the Chinese people in Taiwan. In 1949 the Nationalist Government moved to Taiwan together with two million people from the mainland. Since then Taiwan has been under the military protection of the United States under the Mutual Defense Treaty signed in

1954. Because of the Treaty, American military, government officials, counselors in various fields, businessmen, and missionaries have been stationed in Taiwan. The American culture has been introduced to the Chinese people through personal contacts, mass media, magazines, books, and especially the motion pictures and televisions. The characteristics of the western culture, such as individual freedom, sex equality, and democracy, have been exposed to the Chinese.

However, the dominance of the sex hierarchy has continued to exist to be perpetuated in Taiwan. Therefore, the discrepancies between the ideal structure of sex equality and the actual structure of sex hierarchy have been observed in Taiwan even in the 1960's and 1970's; and they were examined in the following areas: 1) The Status of Women in the Family; 2) The Freedom of Marriage; 3) The Freedom of Divorce and Remarriage; 4) Opportunity to Receive Education and Employment.

The Status of Women in the Family

According to the constitution of Nationalist China, women have the same opportunities in education as do men and have full civil liberties and political equality (2, p. 446). The Civil Code of 1930, the family law of Nationalist China, guarantees for women the right to own property, to inherit family property, freedom of marriage, and the right to become head of the family (7, pp. 125, 355-358) and guardian of children and family property (7, p. 186).

However, the Civil Code is still influenced by the traditional ethics which is still a dominating social force in the society in Taiwan as regards patriarchal dominance, patrilineal family descent, and patrilocalism after the marriage of sons. Therefore, based on the Civil Code, status as head of the family will automatically belong to a senior male member first if there is no other specific method of selection. However, the female can become the head of the family if a senior male member is not available, or that may happen by some special method of selection (7, p. 358). Such a law reveals the impact of the patriarchal system of the traditional family. Besides, after divorce, the children stay with the father instead of the mother (7, p. 184), a fact which shows the impact of the patrilineal descent in the traditional family. Also, when there is disagreement in important family affairs, the decisions of the father will be sustained and become final (7, p. 185)--another impact of the transformed patriarchal dominance.

In the Civil Code of 1930, women still occupy a secondary position in the family. This is evident in three ways (7, p. 113). First is the relationship between the husband and the wife: the wife has to add the surname of the husband on her name (Article 1000); the husband has the right to decide on the place of residence (Article 1002); the husband, being the head of the family, has the right to use and manage the property of the wife (Article 1019, 1043). However, the father is the breadwinner of the family (Article 1026). Secondly, there is the relationship with the children. Children who are under the legal age should reside with the father (Article 1060) and should adopt the surname of the father (Article 1059). The father has precedence over the mother in matters of management of the children's property (Article 1088). Thirdly, there are the kinship relations--when the husband dies and the wife marries again, her relationship with the first husband's family terminates; on the other hand, if the wife dies and the husband marries again, his kinship relations with his deceased wife's family continues (Article 971). In the kinsmen's council, the patrilineal descent precedes the matrilineal descent (Article 1311).

However, Tai Yen-Hui, an authority in law and former law professor at the National Taiwan University and also the President of the Judicial Yuan (branch or department) in Nationalist China, commented that the inequality between husband and wife was even greater in their family life than in the Civil Code. He asserted that the achievement of equality between husband and wife cannot be reached by law alone. More importantly, it is necessary to elevate the status of women, something which will depend on further awakening and effort of women themselves (7, p. 112).

The Freedom of Marriage

The freedom of marriage of the female is guaranteed by the Civil Code. Persons should have free will to choose their marriage partners, and no third party should arrange for or coerce a person to marry against his or her wishes (7, pp. 40-41). Although the freedom of marriage is guaranteed by the Civil Code, the practice of arranged marriage and marriage by purchase still existed in the rural areas in Taiwan in the 1960's. A study was conducted by the Sociology Department of National Taiwan University on marriage and on family problem cases of the Taiwan Provincial Women's Association in Taipei, Taiwan, between 1961-65. Out of 899 cases, 114 were marriage problem cases. Most of the clients (female) were between the ages of twenty and twenty-five years (48.1 percent), and between fifteen and twenty years (25.4 percent). Only 30 percent reported their occupations, but among those reported were peasants, industrial workers, and service occupations such as waitressing (9, pp. 140-141).

The causes of marriage problems were many, and sometimes there were more than one. The main cause was the parental interference with the daughter's marriage. Of 33.9 percent of all the cases, the father's interference constituted 21.3 percent and that of the mother 12.6 percent. About one-fifth of the clients were unwilling to accept engagements which had been arranged for them by their parents, or by others, against their own wills (9, p. 142).

From the above research, one can observe that the freedom of marriage has been jeopardized by the daughters' parents. Such a report revealed that parentally-arranged marriage still existed in Taiwan, and only some of the girls who dared to reject the parental arrangement admitted it publicly. There probably are many more such cases not known by the public.

Freedom of Divorce and Remarriage

The freedom of divorce and remarriage is guaranteed by the Civil Code of Nationalist China. In traditional China only the husband and his parents had the right to bring about a divorce. In Nationalist China, the grounds for divorce include many of the same causes found in the western codes: bigamy, adultery, mistreatment by spouse, abandonment, threat of killing, incurable diseases, mental illness, desertion, and long term imprisonment (7, pp. 160-171). However, there is a cause for divorce which is peculiar and unique in the Civil Code of Nationalist China---mistreatment of wife by the blood relatives and older generations of the husband (Article 1052, section 4). The article states that when treatment of the wife by the blood relatives and the older generation of the husband is such that she cannot tolerate it and live together with them any longer, she can apply for a divorce herself, although her parents or parents-in-law could file for a divorce on her behalf (7, p. 166). This provision is related to the patriarchal and patrilocal concept in Nationalist China.

To trace some of the causes of family problems which may lead to divorce, the same study by the Sociology Department of National Taiwan University on the family problem cases of the Taiwan Provincial Women's Association was again used. From these family problem cases, the social structure in the family in Nationalist China could be seen. Among 785 cases, the causes of family problems are distributed as follows: mistreatment by the husband, 50 percent; negligence of support, 15 percent; mistreatment by the mother-in-law, 3.4 percent, by father-in-law 1.4 percent (9, p. 146). However, only seven percent of the clients ended up in divorce (9, p. 146). There was 28 percent who were between twenty-five and thirty years of age, 21 percent who were between twenty and twenty-five years, and 20 percent who were between thirty and thirty-five years (9, p. 144).

O'Hara made a study of divorce in Nationalist China. There were 223 divorce cases reported in 1954 and 265 cases in 1965 (6, p. 126). In 1965, about eight percent of divorces occurred in the first two years after the marriage and over thirty-five percent occurred in the first five years of married life (6, p. 125). The causes of divorce were bigamy, adultery, mistreatment by spouse and relatives, abandonment, threat of killing, illness, mental illness, desertion, imprisonment, and others. Instances of initiation of divorce by men had increased from 17.3 percent in 1948 to 35.47 percent in 1966. On the other hand, instances of initiation by women had decreased from 82.7 percent in 1948 to 64.15 percent in 1966 (6, p. 127). There is perhaps a hidden factor which accounts for the statistics showing a low rate of divorce in Taiwan. The married couple who agreed to a divorce could go to see a lawyer who would draw up a divorce contract. The couple both signed it, and the divorce was usually not reported to the government, at least for a long time. Also some types of divorces were very inexpensive and frequently funds for support were not sought. That would permit some secrecy (6, pp. 126-127).

However, the number of divorce cases in Taiwan in 1965 was 4,840, based on the demographic census published in 1975 (5, p. 1011). The number of divorce cases increased very little each year, in spite of increase of population and industrialization in the past decade. In 1974, there were 6,766 divorce cases in Taiwan with a population of 16 million people (5, p. 825).

In rural Taiwan, only 1.2 percent of marriages ended in separation or divorce out of 171 major marriages, according to an anthropological study in a rural village (10, p. 183). In the same study, it was noted that young widows without children were urged to stay with their parents-in-law, and the parents-in-law might try to find a man

to marry into the family. Virtuous widows in poor farm families were
filial widows and would stay with the parents-in-law for the rest of
their lives (10, p. 201). In rural areas, the parents still arranged
most of the engagements and marriages of their children. Only a few
young people selected a spouse by free choice and romantic love (10,
p. 101).

The crude divorce rates for Taiwan area was 0.38 percent in 1965
and 0.43 in 1974 (5, p. 1011). Remarriage was also recorded among the
demographic statistics. In 1974, there were 4,31 remarriages among
men and 4,611 among women; and the remarriage rate was 23.8 for men
and 12.0 for women; and in Taipei municipality, the rate was slightly
higher (5, p. 825).

The statistics above show that Taiwan divorce and remarriage rates
are still very low when compared with those of the western societies
and suggest that the traditional family structure still has considerable influence on the contemporary family in Taiwan. The present family
structure appears to be still very stable, and the influences of the
western kinship relations and family structure are not clearly apparent.

Opportunities to Receive Education and
Employment

In traditional China, women were deprived of the opportunities to
receive formal education and gainful employment. However, the Nationalist Government has a policy different from that of the traditional
China, and it claims that the status of Chinese women has improved
steadily since the establishment of the Republic in 1912. Women are
given equal opportunity in education, full civil liberties, and political equality (1, p. 446).

Securing opportunity to receive higher education in Taiwan is
highly competitive. The student population in Taiwan, according to
the Chinese Ministry of Education, was as follows: in 1972 there were
1,266,869 boy and 1,192,874 girl students in elementary schools; in
1971 there were 202,748 boy and 186,497 girl students graduated from
elementary schools (4, pp. 52-54). In 1972 there were 641,525 male
and 464,241 female students in secondary schools, and 122,181 male and
74,970 female students in senior high schools (4, p. 68). In 1971,
there were 30,718 male and 18,886 female students graduated from senior
high schools (4, p. 74). In 1972 there were 158,861 male and 92,197
female students in universities and colleges (4, p. 100) and in 1971
there were 25,136 male and 15,620 female students graduated in universities, colleges and junior colleges (4, p. 106). In 1972 there
were 1,242 male and 907 female students studying abroad (4, p. 156).
From the given statistics, the ratio of male to female students appear
to be 3 to 2 in secondary and higher education. Girls in the families
of the tradition-bound, less-educated, and lower strata were in a dis-
advantageous position because of the low status of the female in tradition. Girls from such families were often denied the opportunity for
further education and are sent to secure employment as soon as the
compulsory education is finished after junior high school (10, p. 93).

The Government of Nationalist China seemed to be proud of the success of the female students in academic achievements and thus to show

the steady ascendency of women's status. In a speech, Madame Chiang Kai-Shek at Chung-Shan Hall, on September 28, 1972 in celebration of Confucius birthday and Teachers' Day (for outstanding teachers), pointed out that in July 1972, a total of 22,767 high school graduates passed the annual joint entrance examinations for twenty-three senior colleges and universities in Taiwan. That was twenty-seven percent of the total candidates. Most of the successful candidates in liberal arts and law were female. All of the thirty-six students enrolled in the history department of National Taiwan Normal University were female. Among the thirty-six students majoring in geography, twenty-nine were female, and of the one hundred studying Chinese literature, eighty-one were female (1, p. 20).

TABLE I

NUMBER OF STUDENTS IN UNIVERSITIES AND COLLEGES
BY FIELDS OF STUDY AND SEX IN TAIWAN, 1971

| Fields of Study | Numbers of Students | |
	Male	Female
Humanities	7,667	16,434
Education	12,567	12,915
Fine Arts	5,593	2,667
Law	2,159	1,076
Social Sciences	37,001	41,744
Natural Sciences	10,460	2,864
Engineering	64,785	1,159
Medical Sciences	10,401	11,225
Agriculture	8,228	2,113

The number of male and female students in diverse fields in the universities and colleges in Taiwan in 1972 are shown above. The Ministry of Education in Taiwan published the table (4, p. 102).

In Table I, the number of female students exceeds the male students only in humanities and social sciences by a large margin. They were about equal in number in education and medical sciences. However, the male students exceeded the female students in law, natural sciences, engineering and agriculture.

In the traditional Chinese society, the women performed the role of housewife and was not supposed to secure gainful employment outside the home. However, the influence of the western culture for the past sixty years, Chinese women have changed and have begun to secure gainful employment outside the family in Nationalist China.

The status of Chinese women has improved steadily since the establishment of the Chinese Republic in 1912 and equality is guaranteed by the Constitution; to assure this, women are guaranteed ten percent of all elective offices (2, p. 317). The Nationalist Government wanted to prove this by pointing out that women work in government organizations, serve in the armed forces, engage in social work and enter the professions. There are women judges, administrators, diplomats, doctors, attorneys, school principals and postmasters. Tens of thousands of women are teaching at all levels, including more than 600 on the faculties of colleges and universities. In the legislative bodies at all levels, there are 52 women in Legislative Yuan (department of branch), 16 in the Control Yuan, 205 in the National Assembly. There are also many female representatives in provincial and county assemblies and city councils (2, p. 317).

When the National Government established the ideal of equality for women in education and employment in Taiwan, an American critic asserted that the Nationalist Government discriminated against women in various occupations and exploited the female sex (3). The Nationalist Government was criticized as a fascist military organization and Taiwan as a man-dominated society (3).

But do ideal and actual structure well coincide? In recent years, the Nationalist Government has produced very detailed statistical reports and the employment of women can be examined. If women were allowed to secure gainful employment outside the family, such a phenomenon would be a deviation from the traditional family structure, and it would have considerable impact on her status in the family.

Based on the statistical reports, the occupational groups by sex can be compared in Table II (8, pp. 63-68). From Table II, one can see that there were approximately twice as many male professional workers as there were females. The ratio was fourteen-to-one in managerial work. The ratio was three-to-two for clerical workers. That category of work included clerical supervisors and bookkeepers and government executive officials which demanded men's service (8, p. 63). There were two men to one woman in sale and service work, as well as in agriculture and production work. Of course, agriculture and production work require considerable physical strength.

It would be interesting to break down the first two occupation groups because they require professional training and have considerable prestige and status in society. From Table III, the number of females came close to that of males only in the categories of medical, dental and related work and in teaching. Women were far behind in the occupations of scientists, engineers, statisticians, mathematicians, economists and jurists.

The managerial workers are important and influential people in society and in Table IV, a comparison is made between the two sexes. The ratio of men to women is 10-to-1 in the leadership positions in Taiwan when men were thirteen times as women in the positions of public and private enterprise managers.

Also, it would be interesting to know the age bracket of the employed female population in the Taiwan Area. Table V is the number and rates of economically active and inactive population aged 15 and over by age and sex for cities and counties of the Taiwan Area, at the

TABLE II

EMPLOYED PERSONS BY INDUSTRY AND OCCUPATION GROUP
BY SEX IN TAIWAN, 1975

Unit: Thousands*

Industry and Occupation Group	Males	Females
Professional, technical and related workers	185*	99*
Managerial workers	115	8
Clerical and related workers	302	196
Sales workers	447	207
Service workers	193	115
Agricultural, forestry, animal husbandry workers, fishermen and hunters	1,091	481
Production workers and transportation, equipment operators and laborers	1,455	580

TABLE III

PROFESSIONAL, TECHNICAL AND RELATED WORKERS
BY SEX IN TAIWAN, 1975

Unit: In Thousands

Occupation Groups	Male	Female
Scientists, engineers and related technicians	46	1
Medical, dental, veterinary and related workers	27	26
Statisticians, mathematicians, economists, system analysts and related technicians	9	0
Jurists	7	0
Teachers	74	65
Authors, journalists and related writers	6	1
Artists and related workers not elsewhere classified	17	5

TABLE IV

MANAGERIAL WORKERS BY SEX IN TAIWAN, 1975

Unit: In Thousands

Occupation Groups	Male	Female
People's representatives and government, administrative chiefs	10	0
Public and private enterprise managers	105	8

TABLE V

EMPLOYED POPULATION BY AGE AND SEX IN TAIWAN
END OF 1974

Age Group	Sex	
	Male	Female
15-19	422,735	378,932
20-24	713,649	414,762
25-29	509,185	218,858
30-34	473,368	188,149
35-39	436,796	184,753
40-44	453,684	169,598
45-49	467,797	136,336
50-54	352,760	97,359
55-59	231,389	62,556
60-64	159,273	40,520
65+	116,764	25,452

end of 1974 (5, pp. 186-187). From Table V, one can see that the employed female population reached its peak in the 15-19 year groups and 20-24 year age groups. It dropped to half of the latter in the 25-29 age groups.

The age group of 20-24 had the highest number of first marriage for female, 69,797; followed by the 15-19 age group with 29,415; and the 25-29 age group with 18,179 (5, p. 797). It is evident that about half of the employed female population dropped out from the labor force after their marriage. However, those who did not drop out from the labor force have stayed on with their work quite steadily.

Comparing the economically active population with the economically inactive population of women aged 15 and over, it is found that total economically active population for female was 1,991,160, which included the employed and the unemployed population (5, p. 186), while the economically inactive population for female was 2,761,818, which included 2,188,879 housekeepers and 435,459 students and the others (5, p. 186-187). So, there were more females as housekeepers than there were females who have gainful employment outside the family. The housekeepers started to appear in large number in the 20-24 age group in the economically inactive population.

Summary and Discussion

Ideally speaking, women should have the equal status with men in Nationalist China since it is guaranteed by the constitution and the Civil Code and the Nationalist Government promised to work towards this direction (2, p. 446). But, in reality, women did not have such equal status.

Women already have had a secondary status based on the Civil Code and they actually do not have the equal privileges as men in the family (7, p. 112). Even worse, the inequality between men and women was greater in the actual family living than the family structure written in the Civil Code (7, p. 112). In other words, in the actual family life inequality for women has been even greater than the ideal kinship relations in the Civil Code.

Ideally, freedom of marriage, divorce and remarriage are guaranteed to women and such freedom gained more ground in urban areas. In rural areas, parental arrangement for daughters' marriage has still been practiced among the peasants and among the laboring class even in urban areas (9, 10).

Ideally speaking, women are given equal opportunities in education and employment, as even the Nationalist Government has supported the policy of sex equality (2, p. 317). But, in reality, parents still preferred to send boys rather than girls to go to school as the student population showed the ratio of three to two for male to female students (4). In gainful employment outside the family, men have had two times as much chance of being employed as have women, and women have not held important positions of leadership (8, pp. 63-68).

Since the Nationalist Government has not enforced the ideal family structure for sex equality in the Civil Code and has left the choice to people to work out their family structure, the ideals in the Civil Code therefore have not been fully realized. Perhaps the political leaders in Nationalist China have still supported the traditional ethics and kinship relations which gave men a dominating position in society and in the family. On the other hand, women might not have been active enough to raise their status to achieve equality.

BIBLIOGRAPHY--CHAPTER VI

1. *China Yearbook 1972-73*, Taipei, China Publishing Co., 1973.

2. *China Yearbook 1975*, Taipei, China Publishing Co., 1975.

3. Daimond, Norman, "Women Under Kuomingtang Rule Variations on the Feminine Mystique," *Modern China*, Vol. I, No. 1, January 1975, 3-45.

4. Ministry of Education, Republic of China, *Educational Statistics of the Republic of China*, 1973, Taipei, Taiwan, 1973.

5. Ministry of the Interior, Republic of China, *1974, Taiwan-Fukien Demographic Fact Book, Republic of China*, Taipei, Taiwan, 1975.

6. O'Hara, Albert R., *Social Problems: Focus on Taiwan*, Taipei, Mei Ya Publications, 1973.

7. Tai, Yen-Huei, *Family Law of China*, Taipei, Cheng Wen Printing Co., November 1970. 6th ed.

8. Taiwan Provincial Labor Force Survey and Research Institute, *Quarterly Report on the Labor Force Survey in Taiwan, Republic of China*, No. 50, Taipei, Taiwan, Jan. 1976.

9. Ting, Polly P.Y. Chi and Mei-Lein Huang, "The Statistical Analysis of Marriage and Family Problem Cases of the Taiwan Provincial Women's Association," *Journal of Sociology*, National Taiwan University, Taipei, April 1967, 137-152.

10. Wolf, Margery, *Women and the Family in Rural Taiwan*, Stanford, Stanford University Press, 1972.

CHAPTER 7

THE RISING STATUS OF WOMEN IN
COMMUNIST CHINA

In this chapter, the sex hierarchy in Communist China is examined. When the Communists took over the China Mainland in 1949, they tried to change the traditional family structure which was patriarchal, patrilineal, and patrilocal. The Communists saw many of the weaknesses and shortcomings of the traditional family, such as inequality of, and discriminations against, women. Besides, the Communists want the people, including women, to put the interests of the nation above those of the individuals and the family; also the labor force of women is needed to reconstruct the country.

Since Communist China is a totalitarian state and a restricted society, it is impossible for social scientists from outside to conduct sociological studies there. Therefore, the method chosen for this study included a thorough review of literature and interviews with informants. Data for this chapter were collected mainly from literature published in Communist China. Data on the ideal family structure in sex status were collected from seventeen articles published in five periodicals (2-7, 10, 13-16, 18, 19, 22, 23, 27, 28) which are official organs of the Communist Government. Data from four newspapers were included as they have been official organs of the Communist Government (8, 9, 24, 26). Since only the official organs of the Communist Government can publish the directives and policies of the nation, they have been the only sources on the ideal family structure.

Data on the actual family structure were collected from two articles published in a periodical (16, 23) and four articles (9, 12, 20-21) published in three newspapers which are official organs of the Communist Government.

Conflicting evidences were found among the data collected among those on the ideal family structure on sex equality and the actual family structure on the sex hierarchy. The Communists openly admitted that they have not completely succeeded on changing the family, geared to their family model, especially in rural areas; and there are people who have not followed and adopted the values, ideology, and normative patterns the national government initiated and taught (9; 16, pp. 5-6; 23, pp. 6-7).

When the Communists started to change the sex hierarchy in the family, they had to fight against the traditional ideas and practices in the family which have perpetuated for the past two thousand years. The goal which the Communists have tried to achieve has been to eliminate the sex hierarchy in the family and society. They have used ideological indoctrinations and models to socialize the people, especially women.

In this chapter, the following areas are examined. 1) New Conceptions of Marriage: Mate Selection, Marriage Age and Marriage Ceremony, 2) Freedom of Divorce and Remarriage, 3) The New Status and Roles of Women.

New Conceptions of Marriage: Mate Selection, Marriage Age and Marriage Ceremony

In traditional China, the most important purpose for marriage was to perpetuate the family lineage and to make the family the center of loyalty. When the Communists began to change the family, they tried to shift the center of loyalty from the family to the nation. Such changes included the criteria of mate selection, which put political ideology in the first place, raising the marriage age, which could lessen the dependence of the daughter-in-law on the parents-in-law, and marriage ceremony, which the Communists tried to make a politically-oriented exercise. The Communists have viewed marriage in traditional China as feudalistic, based on "arbitrary and compulsory arrangements," and they have held that it emphasizes "the supremacy of men over women and in disregard of the interests of the children (1, p. 1). In contrast to tradition, the Communists state that marriage in Communist China is based on "the free choice of partners, on monogamy, on equal rights for both sexes, and on the protection of the lawful interests of women and children" (1, p. 1).

The rights and duties of husband and wife are stated in The Marriage Law, in Chapter III, Articles 7 to 12 (1, p. 3).

ARTICLE 7
    Husband and wife are compansions living together and enjoy equal status in the home.

ARTICLE 8
    Husband and wife are in duty bound to love, respect, assist and look after each other, to live in harmony, to engage in productive work, to care for their children and to strive jointly for the welfare of the family and for the building up of the new society.

ARTICLE 9
    Both husband and wife have the right to free choice of occupation and free participation in work or in social activities.

ARTICLE 10
    Husband and wife have equal rights in the possession and management of family property.

ARTICLE 11
    Husband and wife have the right to use his or her own family name.

ARTICLE 12
    Husband and wife have the right to inherit each other's property.

With regard to the choosing of a mate, the Communists try to educate the people to put the revolution and the country first. The editor of the Worker's Daily, a newspaper, points out what are the conditions for selecting a mate: political attitude, the aim in life, and the outlook in life and the object of affection. A person must not base the choice of mate on beauty or wealth. The editor warns that the youths should not base their choice of a partner for life-long companionship on bourgeois considerations, such as that some girls want a husband with a good salary so that they can live better after marriage. The editor asserted that the important factors are compatibility in ideology and aim in life. Beauty and wealth are fleeting, but an ideology remains forever (26).

The editor elaborated on other considerations on mate selection. For example, consideration should be given not only to ideology, but also to the temperament, age, and feelings of the person. These considerations must be practical and not overly demanding. Temperaments and attitudes need not be the same but they should be compatible for marriage life to be blissful. The best way to get to know each other is in daily working and living. Work closely with each other and discuss things. Naturally this should not interfere with production. Put production and work in the first place. In dealing with love and marriage, youths must be guided by Communist morality (26).

Other detailed discussions and debates on the standard for selecting a mate were published in Chinese Women. In the May and June issues in 1964, the magazine published some letters from its readers, and the editor also gave answers to the questions.

In response to the question of what are the conditions for selecting a mate, the editor expressed the idea that the revolutionary life view should be used in facing the problem of love. She pointed out that among the young people in China at that time there existed the dilemma of possessing a double standard as some youths tried to possess the ideals and ideology of communism and revolution and at the same time tried to live a life of the bourgeoisie in their love affairs (2, p. 27). For the proletariat, standards for selecting a mate should be based on the ideal of revolution--good performance in work, in learning, and in progress in political ideology. So, in selecting a mate, a Communist youth should put the political ideology as the most important requirement for the other party, as well as for oneself to meet. One should require that the other party "know how to live," which means to have good time in leisure and recreation and in love. Some young girls require the other party to be generous, to show loving care, to know how to have a good time and enjoy life so that they will not live a monotonous and bored life. (This kind of social and cultural life was in the subordinate position in scale of importance and for the purpose of recreation (2, p. 27).

Some young people demanded that their mates have the combination of the thought of the proletariat and the lifestyle of the bourgeoisie. The editor denounced such a demand, asserting that such a combination is just not proper. If a young man were steeped in the romantic love and warmth in the family, what would be his attitudes towards the revolution? He would avoid or seek to escape from a revolutionary style of life, would be indifferent to the socialistic revolution and constructions, lacing the necessary interests and sentiment to support

them. If a young person has fallen into the bourgeois style of life,
he will start to grow in the ideology of the bourgeoisie. If any person tries to live the bourgeois style of life and at the same time
wants to possess the ideology of the proletariat, he is using the latter as a camouflage for his pursuit of the former. If a young woman
only demands that her mate has a sound ideology of the proletariat and
depends on him for his support from his high salary, she has debased
herself by taking a subordinate and dependent position (2, p. 28).

The present writer interviewed three educated refugees in Hong
Kong, and they observed that among the common people occupation, income and education were the most important criteria for a woman to use
to choose her mate. Age, political background, and appearance were
next. For a man, criteria for selecting a woman would be her education, income, age and appearance (11). At least as far as such a
limited source of information is used, one can conclude that the actual
criteria among the common people might be quite different from the
ideals the Communists taught.

When the Chinese Communists took over the China Mainland in 1949,
the marriage age, in addition to mate selection, became an issue for
discussion since the Communists want the young people to delay their
marriage, perhaps because of the population problem on the China Mainland. In any case, a considerable amount of propaganda and pressure
have been applied to this issue.

One of the reasons for late marriage was expressed by a professor
of physiology and of medicine, Yeh Kung-Shao, of the Peking Medical
School, in his opinion of the marriageable age and childbirth. When
he replied to letters from the readers of the Chinese Women magazine,
Yeh said that for the youths who were not yet married, he recommended
that they adequately extend their time to stay single. The comparatively ideal age for marriage was twenty-three years for females and
twenty-five to twenty-nine for males. However, this was not inflexibly
specified. It remained necessary to consider each individual's particular situation (28, p. 43).

Communists' attempt to change the family has also included change
in the wedding ceremony. They tried to use their models to educate
the people. An article published in the Chinese Youth Daily described
a new wedding ceremony in Hunan Province. The couple to be married
decided not to follow the traditional style of wedding ceremony. The
bride refused to be carried in a bridal sedan chair to her husband's
home, wishing to save the laboring power needed in farm production.
Her mother did not agree because she believed that if there were any
disputes in the future, her daughter would have no protection since
she walked to her husband's home. (Since there was no marriage registration in traditional China, the bridal sedan chair, the wedding ceremony and feasts were used as proof of a legal marriage). However, the
bride replied to her mother that since their marriage would be registered in the local government, the marriage certificate would be the
best proof. Also, they refused to ask for a fortune-teller to come to
select a "lucky" day for their marriage. In the wedding ceremony that
finally took place, the couple bowed three times to the portrait of
Chairman Mao Tse-Tung. The close relatives had a simple dinner in
their home that night (8).

A similar story was recorded in Fukien Province. A young couple walked fifteen lis (Chinese miles) from the bride's home to the bride-groom's home. She refused to ride on a bridal sedan chair. She just dressed in simple dresses, and the couple still went to work on their wedding day. In the wedding ceremony, they bowed three times to the portrait of Chairman Mao Tse-Tung and also bowed three times to their parents, relatives and friends. The political government officials and all the people from the village came to their wedding. The government officials spoke at the ceremony as well as did the married couple, who encouraged each other in their labor production. Candies, peanuts, beans, and tea were served to the guests, replacing what in earlier times would have been a big feast. The wedding ended with all singing revolutionary songs together. Three days after their marriage, the bride started working again. The old custom was that a bride could not start working until a month after her marriage (9).

There were several implications in this article. The couple first bowed three times to the portrait of Chairman Mao Tse-Tung and then to their parents, relatives and friends. It seemed to imply that the Communist Party wanted the Chinese people to put their political leader in the first place, above the place of their parents and family. It was the Party and its leaders to whom they should owe their first allegiance. In the traditional marriage, the married couple bowed to the groom's parents. The act of bowing to the portrait of Mao and then to their parents, relatives, and friends also implied that they were humble and respectful to others.

When the speaking began, the political officials spoke first in the ceremony, and then later the married couple spoke. It was in contrast to tradition that a political official should speak in a wedding ceremony. Rather, since in tradition a wedding ceremony was a familial, not a political affair, a senior family member should officiate and speak. The new ceremony implied that the government officials were to take over as the family head. Even more contrasting was that the wedding couple encouraged each other in their effort to production. According to the traditional Chinese wedding custom and ceremony, the wedding couple, especially the bride, would keep quiet, and the bride would be very shy and not allowed to say anything. Finally, the wedding couple said before that their marriage was their own business and was not arranged by their parents. It was the wedding couple, not their parents, who were the hosts of the ceremony. They were running their own wedding. Thus, there was urged a revolt against the age hierarchy and the dominance of the parents. The Communists' style of wedding ceremony seemed clearly to have political overtones. It is clear this is what the Communists wanted it to have.

Another important custom in marriage which the Communists sought to change is that of giving a betrothal gift, a certain amount of money or material goods which the bridegroom's family had to pay to the family of the bride. In order to eliminate this custom, an editorial was written in the Chinese Youth Daily in 1964 to explain why the custom of receiving betrothal gifts was wrong and to indoctrinate the youths to abandon that custom. The editor identified the asking for and receiving of betrothal gifts as a custom in the traditional society in which women would be purchased as if they were commercial goods. Some parents wished to make money by asking for a betrothal gift from the groom's family, offering their daughter in marriage. In the tradition-

al society only the wealthy people and rich peasants could afford to
pay for the betrothal gift and many of the poor young men could not get
married because they could not pay for the betrothal gift. Some poor
people borrowed money for the marriage, but were in debt for many
years. The ground for the bride's parents to ask for betrothal gifts
was that since the parents spent so much money and effort to bring up
a daughter, they at least deserve to get something back for compensa-
tion. The editor of Chinese Youth Daily rejected this claim and
claimed instead that it is the duty of the parents to bring up their
children and that the parents should not make claims on their conditions and cost. Since the parents cannot live on bethothal gifts they
receive, everybody has to labor in a Communist society. Even when the
parents are old and unable to work, society will take care of them.
Even when a daughter is married, it does not mean that the parents have
lost relations with her. On the contrary, the daughter and son-in-law
have to give assistance when the parents are in need of help (9).

However, it was said, some young women say that since other people
ask for betrothal gifts, they will lose face if they do not and thus
cannot "show off." The editor said that in the new (Communist) society, it is a shame to waste money unwisely, such as having big feasts,
putting on new clothes, etc., and that, indeed, the girl will lose face
by asking for a betrothal gift, since such a custom is actually the
sale of woman. He strongly urged the local government and political
cadres to help the young people to abolish this feudalistic and capitalistic custom. He asked the local political organization to help to
educate the young women in order to elevate their political awareness
and then to fight against such a bad custom. The young women would be
supported by the Communists in attempting to persuade and to educate
the parents to change (9).

In Fukien province, a young man Lo, Tung-Lin and a young woman
Jen, Chih-Shang fell in love. Both of them were poor peasants, members
of the local militia and model commune members. When they announced
their marriage, the bride's father requested a betrothal gift of three
hundred dollars from the groom's father who could not afford to pay for
it. Lo then told Jen that he was ready to borrow money to pay for the
betrothal gift, but Jen objected to this because the debt would become
a burden to their family life afterwards. She returned home and con-
vinced her parents of the negative results of asking for a betrothal
gift. Her parents then agreed not to ask for a betrothal gift (9).

Another problem appeared because Lo's father decided to have a big
feast for his son's wedding in order to celebrate and to show that
their family had been liberated after the revolution and that the living standards had been raised. Also, since Lo's parents were poor
peasants before the revolution, they had been looked down on by other
villagers because they could not afford to entertain all villagers in
their own wedding twenty years before. The secretary of the local Communist Party branch came to Lo's family and said to the father that to
have a big feast would cost several hundred dollars and that the guests
would have to spend money to buy gifts to come to the feast. The family would go into debt, and it would be much better to save the money
for the improvement of production and for long-term use on the family
living. The father agreed not to have the big feast (9).

There were many more cases of the new marriage ceremony which the

Communists used to educate the young people. A young woman Chi, Fu-Ying in Anhwei province established a new example in her marriage. She objected to her parents asking for dowry from her future husband's family. In order to establish a good example for labor and learning, she asked her parents to give her as wedding gifts the writings of Mao Tse-Tung and instruments for farming, instead of jewels (24). Of course, such gifts are new compared with the expensive and valuable gifts in the traditional marriage ceremony.

Freedom of Divorce and Re-marriage

In Communist China, the freedom of divorce and remarriage is guaranteed in the Marriage Law Promulgated by the Central People's Government on May 1, 1950. In Chapter V Divorce:

ARTICLE 17
Divorce is granted when husband and wife both desire it. In the event of either the husband or the wife alone insisting upon divorce, it may be granted only when mediation by the district people's government and the judicial organ has failed to bring about a reconciliation.

In cases where divorce is desired by both husband and wife, both parties should register with the district people's government in order to obtain divorce certificates. The district people's government, after establishing that divorce is desired by both parties and that appropriate measures have been taken for the care of children and property, should issue the divorce certificates without delay.

When one party insists on divorce, the district people's government may try to effect a reconciliation. If such mediation fails, it should, without delay, refer the case to the county or municipal people's court for decision. The district people's government should not attempt to prevent or to obstruct either party from appealing to the county or municipal people's court. In dealing with a divorce case, the county or municipal people's court should, in the first instance, try to bring about a reconciliation between the parties. In case such mediation fails, the court should render a decision without delay.

After divorce, if both husband and wife desire the resumption of marriage relations, they should apply to the district people's government for a registration of re-marriage. The district people's government should accept such a registration and issue certificates of remarriage.

ARTICLE 18
The husband is not allowed to apply for a divorce when his wife is pregnant, and may apply for divorce only one year after the birth of the child. In the case of a woman applying for divorce, this restriction does not apply.

Since the Marriage Law was promulgated, freedom of marriage a͏ divorce and sex equality have been guaranteed to the people in Co͏ nist China. It is very unusual that the young people seemed to ͏' gotten into a confused and anomic situation relative to their marital affairs under the new Marriage Law, for divorce cases increased drastically in Communist China in the early 1950's. The young people were encouraged and supported by the Communists to break away with the traditional normative pattern based on the ethics and teachings of Confucius on marital affairs. But, at the same time, the young people were not well educated with the new moral standards established by the Communists. Therefore, they were caught in an anomic situation as they did not know what to follow.

After the promulgation of the Marriage Law on May 1, 1950, the number of divorce cases increased significantly throughout the country and reached the peak by 1953 and declined gradually afterwards (21). Comparison can be made between the months before and after the promulgation of the Marriage Law. The Minister of Justice of the Communist Central Government, Shih Liang, a woman, stated that in twenty-one large and medium-size cities, including Peking, from January to April 1950 there were 9,300 matrimonial suits filed and from May to August 1950 the number of divorce cases increased to 17,763 (20).

Seven years after the promulgation of the Marriage Law, Kao I-han of the Judicial Branch, published an article in the People's Daily, entitled "An Analysis of the Changes in Marital Relations at the Present Time" (21). Kao based his analysis on the statistics of the cases compiled by the People's Court of Kiangsu Province for the previous years and upon the investigations based on the random sampling of the judicial branch. The matrimonial suits for marriage formed by traditional arrangement constituted only about seventeen percent of the total number; for marriages formed by parental arrangement, but with the children's consent, they constituted about thirty percent; for marriages formed by free choice, they constituted more than fifty percent. About eighty percent of the applicants for divorce were women. Most of the applicants were young people; forty-nine percent were between 18-25, thirty-six percent were between 20-35. Most of the applicants were recently married; forty percent were married from one to five months, and twenty percent had been married less than a year. About seventy percent of the applicants were granted a divorce by the people's courts (21).

Kao tried to trace the causes for the rapid increase of divorce, and he attributed the primary cause to the changes in the system of production after the establishment of the Communist regime in 1949. Since women had gained economic independence, they did not want to stay in a submissive position in the family any longer. The second cause was the influence of the thought of the bourgeoisie, such as the desire for material enjoyment, prestige, social status, beauty. Among the older group, male supremacy and the restriction of the women in the family also existed. The third cause was the misunderstanding and misinterpretation of the freedom of marriage. Many young people got married in a hurry without serious consideration. Since they could have the freedom of divorce, they needed not consider their marriage seriously.

The third cause constituted the largest number of divorce cases. Although Kao tried to blame the influence of the bourgeoisie as the most important cause of divorce, it actually reflected the failure of the Communist education on marriage since a very large number of the young people still had not accepted their indoctrination on the Communist conditions of mate selection.

In order to show that the high rate of divorce cases existed nationwide, the divorce cases of Heilungkiang province was used for comparison. While Kiangsu province is located in the Southeast of the China Mainland, Heilungkiang is in the northeast of China. An article was written by Liu Cheng-Wen, the President of the Heilungkiang Provincial People's Higher Court in Kuang Ming Daily also in March of 1957 (12). Liu stated that matrimonial cases constituted more than fifty percent of all civil cases and that divorce cases comprised more than ninety percent of all the matrimonial cases. The great majority of the applicants for divorce were between twenty and twenty-five years of age and they married by free choice. Also, most of the husbands and wives were economically independent as most of the young people could earn their own living (12).

Liu then tried to trace the cause of those divorces. The primary cause was that those young people became engaged and married carelessly. After marriage they had not tried to build up their marital relationship. They could and would quickly apply for a divorce if they could not get along. Secondly, the young people had abused their freedom, for some became involved in extra-marital relationships and had then made up a cause for divorce. Thirdly, many of them were misled by the fantasy of romantic love and failed to build up a realistic family life. Fourthly, many of the young couples despised physical labor and were occupied by the desire for material enjoyments. If the demands of material enjoyments were not met, one party would be very upset and would threaten to apply for a divorce (12).

Liu wondered why such non-Communist ideas and high rate of divorce still existed despite the repeated education and propaganda of the Marriage Law in recent years. Liu admitted that the Communists had won a complete victory on destroying the traditional, feudalistic form of arranged marriage in the previous years. But the Communists had not been successful in uprooting the thinking of the bourgeoisie from the people. He therefore suggested those who had abused their freedom of divorce should be punished. Besides, the cadres in the judicial organ lacked correct analysis and studies on the complicated background of those divorce cases and granted a divorce easily on the ground of "intolerable to the suppression of feudalism" on all cases.

Liu also admitted that such an abnormally high divorce rate might be attributed to the shift from the old to the new social order, which included ideology also. He requested the young people to elevate the socialistic consciousness in confronting marriage and family problems. Then he advised the judicial organ to be very careful in handling divoice cases and to make full analysis of the causes through investigation and research. And, education by persuasion should also be applied. Finally, he urged strengthening education for marriage and urged education and criticism of those who took marriage and divorce carelessly (12).

Several implications can be drawn from Liu's article.

1) The Communists showed great concern about the abnormally and unexpectedly high divorce rate after the promulgation of the Marriage

Law in 1950. Such an abnormal phenomenon might be due to the existence of a moral vacuum as the traditional normative pattern was destroyed and the new Communist moral standards had not been well established. Since such a vacuum existed, the material enjoyments were used as a substitute for the moral standard.

2) The Communists had not yet had great achievement in educating the people, the young people in particular, to accept their doctrines, as shown from the high percentage of the youths still occupied by the thinking of the bourgeoisie.

3) The ineffectiveness of the cadres in handling divorce cases without careful investigations and studies and lack of judicial knowledge and experience.

The New Statuses and Roles of Women

The official position of women in Communist China is that it is raised to be equal with that of men. As early as 1927 Mao Tse-Tung commented on the liberation of the Chinese women.

> A man in China is usually subjected to the domination of three systems of authority (political authority, clan authority and religious authority)...As for women, in addition to being dominated by these systems of authority, they are also dominated by the men (the authority of the husband). These four authorities--political, clan, religious and masculine--are the embodiment of the whole feudal-patriarchal ideology and system, and are the four thick ropes binding the Chinese people, particularly the peasants. How the peasants have overthrown the political authority of the landlords in the countryside has been described above. The political authority of the landlord is the backbone of all other system of authority. With that overturned, the clan authority, the religious authority and the authority of the husband all begin to totter... As to the authority of the husband, this had always been weaker among the poor peasant because, out of economic necessity, their womenfolk have to do more manual labor than the women of the richer classes and therefore have more say and greater power of decision in family matters. With the increasing bankruptcy of the rural economy in recent years, the basis for men's domination over women has already been undermined. With the rise of the peasant movement, the women in many places have begun to organize rural women's associations; the opportunity has come for them to lift up their heads, and the authority of the husband is getting shakier every day. In a word, the whole feudal-patriarchal ideology and system is tottering with the growth of the peasants' power (15, pp. 44-46).

If women want to achieve the equal status with men, they must participate in economic production outside the home as does the husband. This was stated by Engels and by Lenin. Engels said: "The emancipation of women and their equality with men are impossible and must remain so as long as women are excluded from socially productive work and restricted to housework, which is private." Lenin also said: "To effect her (woman's) complete emancipation and make her the equal of the man it is necessary for the national economy to be socialized and for women to participate in common productive labor. Then women will occupy the same position as men." (13, p. 17). An article was written in 1974 by Li Chen, a member of the standing committee of the Tientsin Municipal Women's Federation and Chairwoman of the Hoping District Women's Federation in Tientsin, on the Chinese women (13, p. 18). Li states that as long as women remain dependent economically on men and occupy a subservient status, they cannot obtain equality with men politically, socially or in family life. To take part in social labor to achieve economic independence is the necessary basis for women's emancipation (13, p. 21).

Women's participation in politics is strongly emphasized and viewed as absolutely necessary. In an editorial of the People's Daily commemorating the "March 8," International Working Women's Day 1973, the editor states that women's emancipation is a component part of the cause of liberation of the proletariat and the socialist revolution and constructions have succeeded only by the active participation of women. The fundamental tasks for the women's movement are to grasp class struggle and the struggle between the bourgeoisie and the proletariat (16, p. 5). Additional support for the movement was expressed by Lu, Yu-Lan, Deputy Secretary of the Hopei Provincial Party Committee and elected Member of the Party's Central Committee of the Ninth National Congress of the Chinese Communist Party in 1969 (14, p. 10). She said that according to Mao Tse-Tung's teaching on women's emancipation "genuine equality between man and woman can be realized only in the process of socialist transformation of society as a whole." Since the family is a cell of society, only by transforming society can the family be transformed. After women have gained their position in society, changes in family relations will follow (14, p. 10).

As already seen in the teachings about marriage, the status of the wife in the family should be equal to that of the husband. The idea that the wife is dependent on the husband's income for a better living is criticized as a form of social parasitism. The wife should see herself as comrade and co-laborer, equal in status to her mate, and she should develop her ability to aid social construction. If the wife only thinks of herself, she has adopted the capitalistic viewpoint of happiness (10, p. 18).

In the family, husband and wife are equal, both should have a share in family matters, and both should take equal responsibility in house work. A wife in Peking nearly divorced her husband because the husband regarded himself as the boss in the family and his word as law. He looked down on housework as women's business and refused to share doing it. After participating in meetings to criticize Confucius, the husband realized his reactionary ideas of male supremacy and became reconciled with his wife (6, pp. 17-18).

Before the establishment of the people's communes in 1958, there was a debate on whether women must work outside the family. At that time, women were criticized if they did not secure gainful employment outside the family. Chang Yung, Vice-Chairman, all China Women's Federation since 1957 and 3rd Secretary, Women's Work Department, Chinese Communist Party Central Committee in 1957 (25, p. 59), explained the

Communist viewpoint on women's participation in social or household labor. She first explained that women's participation in social labor could be realized only by following the development of socialist construction. For the time being, since the socialist construction had just started, household labor was necessary and adapted to social labor. Women would be fully able to participate in social labor after mechanicalization is further developed (3, p. 1). She emphasized that household labor is indirect laboring for the socialist construction and, as such, should not be looked down upon (3, pp. 1-2). Her third point was that women's participation in social labor should be based on objective as well as subjective conditions. If a woman has the qualifications, if society needs her service, and if she can leave her household chores, then she should participate in social labor. If she does not have all the three conditions mentioned, she should not participate in social labor (3, p. 2).

However, the situation changed after the establishment of the people's communes in 1958. A large number of women, ninety percent of the total women labor force, participated in production (22, p. 17). Since beginning their participation in economic production, women have raised their political consciousness and cultural level (22, p. 18). In order to facilitate women to work outside the family, nurseries and kindergartens were established in large scale (22, p. 18).

The Communists not only encourage women to participate in economic production but also strongly support women's participation in political activities as a profession. In January 1975, the First Session of the Fourth National People's Congress was attended by more than 600 women Deputies from all fields who comprised more than twenty-two percent of the total number of Deputies. Forty-two of the 144 Deputies elected to the National People's Congress Standing Committee were women. One woman out of twelve was appointed Vice-Premier of the State Council and three (out of twenty-two) were elected Vice-Chairmen of the National People's Congress Standing Committee (19, p. 22). Of twenty-nine ministers of the State Council, the Minister of Water Conservatory and Power and the Minister of Public Health are women (18, p. 11). Women hold leading posts in local Party and government organizations at various levels. And 37.9 percent of the cadres in the Peking municipality are women. In addition to the Han nationality, there are more than 10,000 women cadres of Tibetan and other minority nationalities in the Tibetan Autonomous Region (19, p. 22). Women also participate in military affairs as there are women pilots in the Chinese People's Liberation Army Air Force. Wu, Hsiu-Mei, a Deputy Flight Squadron Leader, describes her experience in how she has overcome the traditional idea that women cannot do men's work (27, pp. 10-11). There are women in the militia in the defense of the country (4, pp. 29-34). Women also work in oil extracting in the oil fields (7, pp. 22-27), and on live high voltage transmission electric lines (17, p. 23). In Peking more than forty percent of the scientific and technical personnel are women and in the hospitals thirty-five percent of the senior doctors are women (5, p. 11).

Although the Communists have used a great deal of effort to launch attacks on the sex hierarchy (male supremacy) since the 1960's in the China Mainland, they apparently have not yet achieved their complete victory after a decade of struggle. Madame Soong Ching-Ling, the widow of the late Dr. Sun Yat-Sen, the founder of the Chinese Republic in

1912, and the Vice-Chairman of the Chinese People's Republic since 1959 and Honorary President of all China Democratic Women's Federation since 1950 (25, pp. 585-586), admitted in 1972 that there were people's communes in rural areas where women received less pay than men for equal work in production and that in certain villages patriarchal ideas still had their effect. Proportionately, more boys than girls attended school since parents needed the girls to do household work and would not pay to send the girl to school because of her final departure from the family after her marriage. Before the daughter's marriage, the parents asked for betrothal gifts and a certain amount of money from the future husband's family. Also, the birth of a son in the peasant's family was expected and the birth of a daughter was considered a disappointment. The desire to have at least a son restricted the effect of birth control and planned parenthood. Because of the care for children and household chores, women were prevented from participation in economic production and political activities (23, p. 7). Madame Soong Ching-Ling's comments are mainly on the family of peasants in the countryside.

A year later in 1973, an editorial of the People's Daily commemorating "March 8" International Working Women's Day, also admitted that it was still impossible to eliminate completely the remnants of the old ideas of looking down upon and discriminating against women after China had been under the feudal rule for 2,000 years. The Communists admitted that there had been the evidences of neglecting to train more women cadres and their numbers were far from meeting the needs of the developing revolutionary situation in order to give still better leadership to the masses of women in their advance. A certain percentage of women members should be in leading bodies at all levels. In some factories an unwillingness to accept women as workers was also noted (16, p. 6).

Summary and Discussion

Since the promulgation of the Marriage Law in 1950, the Communists have tried to eliminate the inequality and discriminations against women which were ideal as well as actual family structure in traditional China. As Communist China is a totalitarian state, the central (national) government directs every aspect of the people's livelihood. Therefore, the government has tried to destroy the sex hierarchy in the family and society as well.

In the conceptions of marriage, the Communists try to emphasize sex equality as the ideal kinship relations in marriage and in family living. Both the husband and wife shared the household work together. On the selection of mates, the Communists suggest the political ideology and participation as the first criteria for selection as the ideal. However, the actual structure has been different as occupation and income became the criteria for selection rather than political activism among the common people as reported from the refugees in Hong Kong. Besides, a lot of young people tried to adopt a double standard by having a proletarian ideology and bourgeois style of family living (2, pp. 27-28) which could not coexist as commented by the Communists. The Communists also tried to change and simplify the wedding ceremony and add politics in. Because of the economic condition in China Mainland, perhaps no one could afford to have a big and expensive wedding ceremony and feast as in traditional China. So, it is quite reasonable to believe that the ideal and actual structures could come close. The ideal model of the new style of wedding ceremony, which put politics in priority, has been used by the Communists to educate the young people to follow. However, the overall changes in the wedding ceremony and the raising of the marriageable age have eliminated the subordinate status of women in the family, including the indoctrination on the young girls to refuse to ask for betrothal gifts.

On divorce and remarriage, the ideal of the Communists' expectation is to let the couples married under the traditional arranged marriage to break up their marriage and marry again. But, out of their expectation, there was a low percentage of couples who were married by arranged marriage asked for a divorce; and the Communists felt disappointed (21). Ironically, more than fifty percent of the divorce cases were young couples whose marriages were formed by free choice under the Communist regime (21); and thirty percent of divorce was asked by couples whose marriages were arranged by the parents but with the children's consent (21). Divorce rate rose drastically since 1953, three years after the promulgation of the Marriage Law, and gradually leveled off in 1957 (12). Perhaps such an unusual phenomenon might be attributed to the destruction of the traditional normative pattern in the family and at the same time the new kinship relations have not gained any stronghold. The young married couples were thrown into a period of anomie and did not know which normative pattern to follow.

According to the Communist ideology, in order to achieve equal status with men, women must have economic independence by participation in economic production on one hand; and women must also participate in political activities in order to gain social and political independence on the other. The Communists have tried very hard to achieve this ideal by offering opportunities for women to secure gainful employment outside the family; and women's participation in economic production and political activities have been widespread in Communist China. However, the ideal of sex equality has not been completely fulfilled as discriminations against women still existed, even admitted by Communist leaders in the early 1970's (23, p. 7; 16, p. 6). The Communists believed such a phenomenon was attributed to the deep-rooted traditions in the past.

BIBLIOGRAPHY--CHAPTER VII

1. Central People's Government, The Marriage Law of the People's Republic of China, promulgated on May 1, 1950; Peking, 2nd printing, 1975.

2. Chang, Ta-Pang, "Use the Revolutionary Life Viewpoint to Face the Problem of Love," Chinese Women, Peking, May 1, 1964, 27-28.

3. Chang, Yun, "Let Us Discuss the Viewpoint of Women's Participation in Social or Domestic Labor," Chinese Women, Peking, May 1, 1957, 1-2.

4. "Island Militia-Women," China Reconstructs, Peking, China Welfare Institute, May 1974, 29-34.

5. "Questions People Ask about Chinese Women," China Reconstructs, June 1975, 10-11.

6. "Between Husband and Wife," China Reconstructs, June, 1975, 17-18.

7. "Women's Oil Extracting Team," China Reconstructs, Peking, June 1975, 22-27.

8. Peking, Chinese Youth Daily, January 17, 1963.

9. Peking, Chinese Youth Daily, November 19, 1964.

10. Hu, Pai-Jen, "Happiness Must Be Built on the Basis of Labor," Chinese Women, September 1, 1963, 18.

11. Interviews with three educated refugees in Hong Kong in November, 1972.

12. Peking, Kuang Ming Daily, March 12, 1957.

13. Li, Chen, "Women Take Part in Productive Labor," Peking Review, March 22, 1974, 17-19, 21.

14. Lu, Yu-Lan, "Liberation of Women," Peking Review, March 10, 1972.

15. Mao, Tse-Tung, "Report on an Investigation of the Peasant Movement in Hunan," March 1927, Selected Works of Mao Tse-Tung, March 16, 1973, 44-46.

16. "Working Women Are a Great Revolutionary Force," Peking Review, March 16, 1973, 5-6.

17. Peking Review, March 30, 1973, 23.

18. "Proclamation of National People's Congress of People's Republic of China," Peking Review, January 24, 1975, 11.

19. "Working Women on Various Fronts," Peking Review, March 28, 1975,

20. Peking, People's Daily, October 13, 1951.

21. Peking, People's Daily, March 7, 1957.

22. "People's Commune ... A Very Good Device for the Thorough Liberation of Women," Red Flag, March 1, 1960, 17-18.

23. Soong, Ching-Ling, "Women's Liberation in China," Peking Review, February 11, 1972, 6-7.

24. Hong Kong, Ta Kung Daily, November 18, 1965.

25. Union Research Institute, Who's Who in Communist China, Hong Kong, Union Press, Vol. I and II, 1970.

26. Peking, Worker's Daily, December 6, 1962.

27. Wu, Hsiu-Mei, "Taking to the Skies," China Reconstructs, Peking, March 1975, 10-11.

28. Yeh, Kung-Shao, "On Marriageable Age," Chinese Women, August 1, 1962, 43.

CHAPTER 8

EDUCATION AND THE FAMILY IN TRADITIONAL CHINA BEFORE
1911 AND IN REPUBLICAN CHINA, 1911-49

Education and the family has had close relationship to each other in China, and the relationship was especially strong in traditional China. In this chapter, the relationship between education and the family in traditional China and in Republican China are examined.

The method chosen for this study included a thorough review of literature and careful selection of data. Data were collected from literature published in the U.S.A. and in Nationalist China. From the U.S.A. four books written by four scholars on education (1, 2, 4, 8), including its relations with the family, in traditional China and Republican China published by recognized university presses were selected. From Nationalist China, two books, an official document and an article, were included. Two books, written by two scholars, and published by well-established commercial presses (3,7) were used. Both books elaborated the affinity between education and the family. From the official document of Nationalist China (5), the educational policy of Republican China, which also became the educational policy of Nationalist China, was found. An article was written by an anthropologist on the changes of the Chinese family, which was influenced by education, was published in a professional journal (6).

No conflicting evidences were found among the data as the authors recognized the dominance of the Confucian educational thought in traditional China and observed the collapse of its dominance in Republican China.

Education and the Family in Traditional China

Confucius advocated the use of schools to teach his ethics, just as they were taught at home. Confucius' emphasis on education and kinship relations showed he believed there was a strong affinity between the two elements. The characteristics of the educational thought of Confucius are examined here, with special emphasis on their links with the family.

There were several characteristics of the educational thought of Confucian school which had direct influences on the foundation of the traditional Chinese social order and thus also to the traditional Chinese family.

The first characteristic was that it was based on the rules of kinship relations as its starting point. Confucian educational thought was based on humanism and the individual's cultivation of himself as an ethical being (3, p. 64). The practical purpose for the cultivation of self as an ethical being was that "only after a person has successfully cultivated himself as an ethical being will he know how to manage a household. Only after every household has successfully been managed can the country be said to have been governed well" (4, p. 87). Confucianism linked the cultivation of self as an ethical being and the management of the household and the nation which had become an aspiration, calling, and career for Chinese intellectuals to bear the duty of civil service to serve the nation. However, if a person could not serve his country, he would at least be able to manage his household if he were a patriarch or its candidate. So the Confucian educational thought had its immediate practical utility in the family.

The second characteristic of the educational thought was that it pointed to the direction and formation of social strata and the elevation of mental labor. Mencius (372-289 B.C.), who considered himself a devoted follower of Confucius and who was regarded as the most important philosopher in the development of Confucian ideology (4, p. 3) stated that "some labor with their brains and some labor with their brawn. Those who labor with their brains govern others; those who labor with their brawn are governed by others" (2, p. 9). Thus, the traditional social order was thought to be divided into two social classes. Mencius also said, "If there were no men of a superior grade, there would be no one to rule the countrymen. If there were no countrymen, there would be no one to support the men of superior grade" (2, p. 9). After Mencius had laid down such a standard of social stratification, education became a channel of social mobility and occupations requiring physical labor became looked down upon as inferior. Thus, education also was detached from physical labor.

The third characteristic of the Confucian educational thought was oriented toward civil service. In traditional China, agriculture was the main item of the economy, and the ownership of large quantity of farm land and material goods, as by the landlords and the rich merchants, was the conventional channel of social mobility (7, p. 61). Another channel was through civil service. In order to enter the civil service, a candidate had to pass civil examinations. The examination system itself originated from the Han, the Sui and T'ang Dynasties (3, pp. 159-160).

The examinations were used by the emperors to control the intellectuals as well as to recruit civil servants. Therefore, the emperors had tried to induce the intellectuals to enter the civil service. An emperor in the Sung Dynasty (960-1279 A.D.) stated, "In the book, there are plenty of grains, gold houses, beautiful women and plenty of carriages and horses" (3, pp. 160-161). Indeed, the majority of the intellectuals took education as a means to worldly end for a salary to become rich and for a title in order to be thought of as honorable. All the student had in mind was what success could bring to him in terms of power, influence and prestige, and his father and elder brothers pushed him towards this goal (4, p. 167). The civil service examination system finally was criticized as not being able to produce the type of officials with good character and a sense of righteousness to shoulder the great responsibilities of the country (4, p. 168).

The fourth characteristic of Confucian educational thought was the formation of an elite stratum of the scholar-officials and their status, roles, and influences on society. The scholar-official stratum was a ruling group by virtue of moral superiority and therefore was made up of superior men (2, p. 9). This group of people dominated the social and economic life of the traditional social order and was the stratum from which the official came. Its members were the leaders of the traditional society in all important aspects and were civil leaders, custodians of the Chinese culture, and teachers of the Confucian ethics and philosophy (1, pp. 51-58).

Although the civil service examinations were opened to all the people regardless of their socio-economic background, the family background of the students had a great influence on the success and selection of the candidates. The government did not operate any schools, although it was in charge of the civil service examinations. Therefore, providing education was left to the people. There were several types of private schools: (1) family schools; (2) clan schools; (3) village schools; (4) private academies. Family schools were operated by the official and gentry families wealthy enough to hire a tutor to teach the youths at home. Clan and village schools were operated and financed by the clans and villages respectively and their members could be admitted. A tutor was hired and fees were paid (2, p. 12). Of course, a person could easily see the advantages the students of the wealthy families had over the common people, since better teachers could be employed and the youths could have more time to study without participating in production. Therefore, it was evident that the scholar-official stratum had a much better chance to perpetuate itself from one generation to another.

The letters of Tseng Kuo-Fan, an important scholar-official of the Ch'ing Dynasty, to his sons illustrated the impact of the family on the education of the youths.

> To Chi-tseh, the 21st day of the 4th month, 1859
> Outside of the Four Books and the Five Classics, the books I like most are the Historical Records. Chuang-tze, History of the Han, and Han Yu. My love for them has lasted for more than ten years, but unfortunately I have not had time to study them as thoroughly as I should. Besides I also like the History as A Mirror, Selected Works by Prince Chao-ming, Selected Works in the Ancient Style by Yao Pao-hsi, and finally, Selected Poems from Eighteen Schools, also by Yao Pao-hsi.
> During my younger days when I diligently pursued my studies, I was hoping not only to master these dozen or so books, but also to follow the example of Ku T'ing-lin and Wang Huai-tsu to write commentaries on them. I am not getting old, and being occupied by worldly affairs of the most difficult nature, have not been able to accomplish what I once wanted very much to do. Whenever I think of my failure, I am deeply ashamed. My son, if, besides the Four Books and the Five Classics, you read carefully and think deeply about the eight books which your father loves so much, and then write notes to indicate what you have gained from reading them or what you do not understand, I shall be so happy that I will sleep well every night. This will be the best gift you can give to me (4, pp. 349-350).

> To Chi-tseh, the 14th day of the 1st month, 1861
> Your strokes (calligraphy) are weak; it is advisable

that from now on you should follow the style of Liu Kung-ch'uan... Trace one hundred characters each day so as to imitate his stroke structure and acquire the feel of the original. Each time you write me, enclose a few sheets of your calligraphy for me to examine.

After you finish reading the commentaries on the Commentaries of Tso, you should immediately begin reading History as A Mirror...

I am glad to hear that teacher Teng speaks well of your brother Hung. Since Hung is reading History as A Mirror at the moment, you, being the elder brother, should also teach him from time to time.

Your reading ability is good, and you are also doing well in calligraphy. But your ability to compose, in prose as well as in poetry, is comparatively low. Had you been well instructed in this matter when you were fifteen or sixteen, this shortcoming could have been easily avoided. But you are now twenty-three. The future depends upon your own efforts; your father, brothers, or teachers cannot give you much help. Knowing that composition is your weakest point, you should apply yourself more intensively in this field. Since reading and calligraphy are your strong points, you should still strive to improve them.

Walk with dignity and speak with clumsiness. Can you always remember this instruction? I am well; tell your mother that she should not be worried about me (4, p. 352).

The family had a great influence on the selection and success of a candidate. For instance, Chu-Jen degrees or official position were sometimes granted to sons or grandsons of high government officials, to the persons who detected and reported the rebellions, and to those who contributed money to military fund. Some students got their degree and office through imperial favor without taking the examination (1, p. 183). Besides, the high officials could use influence and pressure on the metropolitan examinations and bribery and corruption were common (1, p. 186).

Education and the Family in Republican China 1911-1949

In the Republican period, the educational thought in China came to a crisis. The traditional Confucian educational thought was under criticism and attack, on one hand, while at the same time a new educational thought was not well established. Although the people found the educational thought in a stage of confusion, the traditional practice of using education as a means for social mobility was not forgotten or abandoned by the parents. Besides, the Nationalist government started sending students to study abroad, and their influences on the nation were crucial. In this section, the relationship and interaction between education and the family are examined.

After the Ch'ing Dynasty was overthrown in the Revolution in 1911, the Republic of China was established. In 1929 the Nationalist government had promulgated the aim of Chinese education, and the supreme target was to realize the Three Principles of the People--nationalism, democracy, and social well-being--created by Dr. Sun Yat-Sen (5, pp.

2, 4). Further, the purpose of Chinese education was "to improve national economic life and to prolong the life of the nation, so that we can attain, by all means, to independence of the nation, democracy and higher standard of living, and in end, advance to an ideal world where harmony and equality prevail" (5, p. 5).

The relationship between education and culture was also discussed and a policy adopted in the Republican period in the National Assembly on December 25, 1946, and it was promulgated by the Nationalist Government on January 1, 1947. It stated as follows: "The nation's educational and cultural services shall have as their aim the development, among the citizens, of national characteristics, democratic spirit, traditional morality, good physique, scientific knowledge, and the ability to earn a living" (5, p. 5). Besides, the influences of the thought of the west, such as individualism, democracy, industrialization and urbanization also had impact on the family (6, p. 10).

First, the emphasis on nationalism had weakened the family as the center of loyalty. The war with foreign powers in the mid-nineteenth century and the early twentieth century and the Anti-Japanese War between 1938-1945 had stimulated the spirit of nationalism of the Chinese people (3, p. 370). Because the Chinese people had been excluded from participation in political activities for the past two thousand years under the imperial rule, the common people lacked the spirit of nationalism. They were only interested in their own livelihood and their family, and that has been especially significant among the peasants in the countryside (3, p. 371).

The second significant influence of education on the family was the change in the nature of social mobility. When the civil service examinations were abolished in 1905, even before the establishment of the Republic in 1912 (2, p. 19), there were other channels for upward mobility, besides entering the civil service, such as entering the professions or doing business (8, p. 502).

The third significant correlation between education and the family was that the opportunity for advanced education was monopolized by the wealthy and the rich. Children of the lower class families, such as the peasants and industrial workers, were deprived of the opportunities for education. Only the rich landlords, merchants, and capitalists could afford to send their children to receive higher education (3, p. 379). Thus, the upper and upper middle classes still monopolized education as they had in historical China. Family background could determine the social status of its offspring, and most likely the children of the upper and upper middle classes could retain the class standing of their family of orientation. Thus, despite the increase in channels of social mobility, the social classes perpetuated themselves.

The fourth significant influence of education on the family and vice versa was material welfare. It was the result of the collapse of the Confucian educational thought and the adoption of the scientific knowledge of the west. Those educators who advocated the modernization of education in China could only copy and emphasize the surface of the west and had not absorbed the real essence of the western civilization, and neglected to observe its social and political aspects and structure (3, p. 437).

105

The many debates about the place and status of the Confucian educational thought and ethics in modern education left a confusion and vacuum in the educational thought in the Republican Period. Some educators suggested abandonment of the Confucian educational thought altogether, and others suggested that the traditional education should be used to cultivate the students' character and western knowledge as an instrument (3, p. 437). However, the material productions by scientific knowledge had also captured the attention of the Chinese. Material welfare had thus become a great attraction.

Other characteristics of the educated elites were their training from abroad and their influences on the government and the nation as a whole. Since its defeat in several wars with foreign powers in the nineteenth century, the government of the Ch'ing Dynasty had been sending students abroad to foreign countries mainly to study military techniques. The national government of the Republican Period also followed the practice of the Ch'ing government and continued sending students to pursue further studies abroad (8).

Summary and Discussion

The Confucian educational thought linked the cultivation of self as an ethical being and the management of the household and the nation. These had become an aspiration and calling for Chinese intellectuals. It also pointed to the direction and formation of social strata and the elevation of mental labor. Also, Confucian educational thought was oriented toward civil service and the formation of an elite stratum of scholar-officials, causing parents to urge and support sons to get an education to advance in status. The sons of the scholar-official had a better chance of getting an education and of passing the civil service examinations. Thus, the families of scholar-officials tended to perpetuate their class standing.

The Confucian educational thought was supported and adopted by the rulers in traditional China in order to control the intellectuals. The civil service examinations were established to recruit and control the intellectuals, since those who passed the examinations would become government officials and be rewarded with wealth, prestige, and power. Because the vast majority of people were materialistic as a whole, the family supported education in traditional China. The educational thought of Confucius, as an ideal at least, could become an actuality through the patronage of the ruler and the support of the family. Indeed, the ideal was very closely identical with the actuality (2, 3, 7).

In the Republican period, the educational thought in China came to a crisis as the traditional Confucian educational thought was under criticism and attack, on one hand, while at the same time a new educational thought was not well established. There were several characteristics in education in this period. The intellectuals chose other channels, such as entering the professions or doing business, for upward mobility, besides solely entering the civil service as in traditional China. The opportunity for advanced education was monopolized by the wealthy and the rich families which could perpetuate their class standing by using education as a means. Material welfare played an important part in the life of the intellectuals. Finally, the Chinese

106

government started sending students to study abroad, and the returning students had important influence and impact on the nation.

When the Three Principles of the People (nationalism, democracy and social well-being) became the ideal social, political and educational thought in the Republican period, perhaps the first principle, nationalism, came closest to being also the reality, among the intellectuals in particular. Education was again monopolized and used by the wealthy families to perpetuate their class standing. Since the civil service was not the only way for social mobility as in traditional China, the relationship between the government and the family through education as a means for social mobility was lessened. The intellectuals could pursue wealth and prestige outside the government service. This perhaps lessened the obligations of the intellectuals to the service of their country and the people.

BIBLIOGRAPHY--CHAPTER VIII

1. Chang, Chung-Li, The Chinese Gentry, Seattle, University of Washington Press, 1967, 3rd printing.

2. Hu, Chang-Tu, ed. Chinese Education Under Communism, New York, Teachers College, Columbia University, 1962.

3. Jen, Shih-Hsien, The History of Chinese Educational Thought, Taipei, Taiwan Commercial Press, 1972. 4th ed.

4. Li, Dun J. ed., The Essence of Chinese Civilization, Princeton, D. Van Nostrand, Inc., 1967.

5. Ministry of Education, Education in the Republic of China, Taipei, The Veteran Printing Press, 1970.

6. Ruey, Yih-Fu, "Changing Structure of the Chinese Family," Bulletin of the Department of Archaeology and Anthropology, National Taiwan University, XVII, XVIII, November 1961. 1-15.

7. T'ao, Hsi-Sheng, Marriage and Kins, Taipei, Taiwan Commercial Press, 1968, 2nd ed.

8. Wang, Yi-Chu, Chinese Intellectuals and the West, 1872-1949. Chapel Hill, University of North Carolina Press, 1966.

CHAPTER 9

EDUCATION AND THE FAMILY IN NATIONALIST CHINA

In this chapter, the relationship between education and the family in Nationalist China is examined. The educational policy of Nationalist China has been the fulfillment of the Three Principles of the People; but in actuality, many students, professionals and their parents have not supported such an ideal.

Data for this chapter were collected mainly from public documents published by official organs of Nationalist China in Taiwan. The ideals of the educational policy of Nationalist China were collected from the publications of the related official department (namely, education) as only the official organs could promulgate the educational policy of the nation (12).

Data on the actual support of the national educational policy by the students, professionals and their parents were collected from literature published by the official organs of the Nationalist Government which only could provide statistics of student population and interpret the educational policy. Therefore, data were collected from five public documents (8-10, 13, 14) and seven articles in a newspaper (1-7) which are official organs of the Nationalist Government. A public document published by a U. S. official organ was included for the purpose of obtaining data on the Chinese students staying permanently in the U.S.A. after the completion of their education (15). Finally, ten Chinese students from Taiwan were interviewed for the purpose of finding out the reasons for their studying abroad and staying permanently in the U.S.A. (11).

Conflicting evidences were found among the data especially on the discrepancies between the ideal of the national policy and the actual support of the students and their parents. The Nationalist Government openly admitted in their literature that in actuality the educational policy of the nation has not been honored and supported by many of her most qualified and needed students, professionals and their parents. One explanation could be that people prefer to be better off rather than worse off materially. Many people would choose to live better off materially than would choose to support an ideal which could cost their material welfare.

When the Communists took over the China Mainland in 1949, the Nationalist Government moved to Taiwan, and it has perpetuated The Three Principles of the People as educational policy in the Republican Period. However, a phenomenon unusual for Chinese has been occurring since the mid-1960's. College graduates, mostly from the middle and upper-middle class families, under the encouragement of their parents, have pursued further studies abroad for the purpose of staying permanently in foreign countries, in the U.S.A. in particular and in Canada, in the early 1970's. The migration of intellectuals to foreign countries caught the attention of the Nationalist Government only in the mid-1970's when the independence in national defense and economic development were urgently needed. In this chapter the contradiction between the national education policy and the desires of the students and their parents will be examined in the following areas: 1) The Educational Policy of Nationalist China, 2) The Movement of Nationalist Chinese Students Studying Abroad.

The Educational Policy of Nationalist China

Since the Nationalist Government moved to Taiwan in 1949, it has perpetuated the aim of education it had established on the China Mainland. The supreme target was to realize the Three Principles of the People--nationalism, democracy, and social well-being--created by Dr. Sun Yat-Sen (12, pp. 2, 4). The education of Nationalist China perpetuates the traditional morality and ethics based on the teachings of Confucius. Therefore, the realization of the Three Principles of the People was and is the primary goal and is supplemented by the traditional ethics and morality.

The Movement of Nationalist Chinese Students
Studying Abroad

Education has continued to be used, as it was earlier, as a channel of social mobility for the reward of wealth, prestige and power, as well as the cultivation of a moral character. By the turn of the century, considerable numbers of Chinese students were sent by the national government to pursue further studies abroad in order to learn the advanced science and technology of the west. However, in the Republican period, besides the government-sponsored students, wealthy families also sent the children, mainly sons, to pursue further studies abroad since the returned students could contribute their new knowledge and service to the country, on one hand, and since there would be rewards of wealth and prestige to the students and their families on the other hand (15, p. 502). Since then, studying abroad has become a desirable and honorable event for the Chinese intellectuals.

From the beginning of the Second World War, the United States was one of the allies of the Chinese Government and has been the military defender of Nationalist China on Taiwan since 1949. Thousands of Americans from different professions were stationed in Taiwan, and the U.S.A. provided large amounts of foreign aids to Taiwan. Because of the close relationship between the two countries and because of the United States' advanced technological development, the pursuit of further studies in the United States has become a commonplace. A large number of Chinese students, about two thousand a year, come to the United States for graduate studies (14, p. 156).

The number of Chinese students studying abroad reached its peak in the late 1960's and has gradually leveled off by the middle of the 1970's. In the late 1960's, the number of Chinese students studying abroad in foreign countries showed a great increase, according to the report of the Ministry of Education in 1970 (12, p. 44). In 1969, 3,444 Chinese students were studying in twenty-one countries and of these 2,213 were men and 1,231 were women. In the following tables,

110

their countries of study and fields of study are listed.

TABLE I

THE NUMBER OF NATIONALIST CHINESE STUDENTS IN
DIFFERENT FOREIGN COUNTRIES IN 1969

Country	Number of Students
U.S.A.	3,015
Japan	122
France	66
Canada	58
West Germany	54
Spain	36
Others	193
Total	3,444

TABLE II

FIELDS OF STUDIES OF THE NATIONALIST CHINESE
STUDENTS IN FOREIGN COUNTRIES IN 1969

Field of Study	Number of Students
Natural Sciences	741
Social Sciences	728
Engineering	717
Humanities	480
Agriculture	397
Art	138
Medicine	116
Law	69
Education	58
Total	3,444

The majority of the Chinese students required financial aid of one kind or another. Students majoring in natural sciences and engineering fields could obtain financial aid from higher education institutions more easily than could others. The American economy has direct influences on the financial conditions of the Chinese students and the recession beginning in the early 1970's prevented many from coming. In 1972, the total number of Chinese students studying abroad dropped to 2,149 and the number of students in the U.S.A. was down to 1,867 (10, p. 320; 14, p. 156).

Reasons for Studying Abroad and Staying Permanently in Foreign Countries

Having associated with the Chinese students from Taiwan for the past ten years, the present writer can point out the several reasons for them to pursue further studies abroad.

One of the reasons is that many of the Chinese students are ambitious and would like to pursue advanced academic studies and higher degrees which they could not receive in Taiwan. As studying abroad could improve a student's academic, professional and socio-economic status, the ambitious ones would pursue further studies abroad. Besides, ambitious parents would add pressures to encourage the less ambitious students to go. Perhaps, also, many were caught up in the movement and just followed what the others were doing. The majority came mainly for the purpose to stay permanently in the foreign countries, in the U.S.A. in particular.

Many of the Chinese students who pursued further studies abroad before 1949 would return to work in China after the completion of their education (16, p. 502). But the students coming from Taiwan do not want to return and prefer to stay in the foreign countries where they have completed their education, especially in the U.S.A. The Immigration Act under President Kennedy's administration in the early 1960's made it possible for new immigrants from Asia to come to the United States in large numbers (15). Perhaps because of the rapid development of the American economy and the shortage of professional manpower during the war in Vietnam, large numbers of Chinese students secured employment and permanent residence visas to stay and work in the United States. The attractions of a good income, suitable job opportunities, and development induced many Chinese students to stay in the United States. The average American daily necessities such as the automobiles and modern air-conditioned house, could be enjoyed only by the wealthy in Taiwan. Besides, job opportunities and salary were limited in Taiwan as well as the settings for further research (10, p. 208). (The present writer taught in Taiwan for six months in 1973 and could compare the difference between the living conditions in the two places.)

The Chinese students from Taiwan who were pursuing further studies and planning to stay permanently were interviewed in 1975 on the relationship of their further studies abroad and the influence of their family (11). They gave the following reasons for their decisions:

1) The family usually encouraged the children to study abroad to receive higher degrees in order to bring glory to the family;

2) Peer group and classmates' pressure to pursue further studies abroad;

3) For those who are ambitious, working in the U.S.A. could provide valuable experience and personal advancement, whereas the opportunities for promotion and advancement in Taiwan were very limited;

4) For those who are materialistically oriented, working in the U.S.A. could provide material enjoyment which a person could not obtain in Taiwan. (The income in the U.S.A. would be eight to ten times more than their income in Taiwan.) (10, p. 208).

5) Because of the uncertainty of the political future of Taiwan, some parents encouraged their children not to return.

The Official Attitudes of Nationalist China Towards the Movement of Chinese Students' Studying Abroad

The great majority of the Chinese students stayed in the United States after the completion of their education, and the Nationalist Government was aware of it. The Ministry of Education stated in 1970 that

> in order to accelerate the development of the economic programs and science education, the Government of the Republic of China has provided some particular regulations in encouraging those Chinese students who completed their studies in other countries to come back to work in their professional fields (12, p. 44).

The Ministry continued saying that "recently we have had more students coming back for work year-by-year, so in the year 1969, the total number of students who came back reached 301 persons" (12, p. 44).

Up to the first few months of 1975, the Nationalist Government seemed to have adopted a policy not to interfere with students pursuing further studies and their permanent residence abroad. However, the political situation changed in April, 1975, and the economic situation in the U.S.A. for the past few years has forced many students to return. The retreat of the United States from Cambodia and South Vietnam in the spring of 1975 shocked many countries in Asia, and many countries realized that they should rely on themselves more. Nationalist China on the island of Taiwan which realized that self-reliance in the development of industry, national economy, and defense was urgently needed. In order to accomplish these objectives, highly trained and skillful personnel and professional people are needed and the thousands of students studying abroad are the ones the government tries to call back (4).

With the death of the late President Chiang Kai-Shek on April 5, 1975, the Nationalist Government has made use of the Central Daily News published in Taipei, an official organ of the Nationalist Party, to launch a series of attacks and criticism on the university students in Taiwan, the students studying abroad, those having made their permanent residence in the U.S.A. after the completion of their education, and the parents of the students also. The articles described the late

President as a national hero and a patriot, who has given his whole life for the survival of the country, in contrast to the attitudes and behavior of the college students.

An article entitled, "An Analysis of the College Students of Today," was published by the Central Daily News, Taipei, Taiwan in early May, 1975. Its writer first pointed out the dangerous political situation of Taiwan, such as the frustrations and setback in foreign diplomacy, the death of President Chiang, and the loss of Cambodia and South Vietnam. He pointed out that Taiwan was in a very serious and dangerous situation, its survival threatened, and that it was even worse than the political situation existing in the 1910's before the outbreak of the May Fourth Movement in 1919. He called upon college students to save the country, but noted that, unfortunately, they seemed interested only in their own personal future and success, a good occupation, and further studies abroad. They lacked independent thinking, imagination, moral convictions and nationalistic consciousness, the author of the article said. Besides, the parents and the elders also taught the young people to be interested in personal success and material benefits, he asserted. Some students were so caught up by the western culture that they could not understand its meanings, and as a result they had given up their Chinese culture. Eventually, this group would go abroad and stay there permanently. Finally, college students were called to bear the responsibility to establish their nationalistic faith and self-confidence to save the country (1).

Another article, entitled "Create A New Era," was published by the Central Daily News in the middle of May, 1975. In it college students were accused of lacking the moral and ethical conviction which is the core of the Confucian educational thought and nationalism and patriotism as it was in the early 1910's in the China Mainland. The author pointed out that the two dangers in Taiwan today were first, egoism and the lack of nationalism, and second, the failure of today's education in which students became only a storehouse of knowledge and were not educated to become a "person." The great majority of students stayed in the U.S.A. after the completion of their education and their excuses were that there were no suitable jobs for them in Taiwan and no suitable environment for doing research. Because most people were interested in themselves and not in the country, the nation was thus not well developed. They put the interests of self above those of the nation. Most students today were only interested to get into the university and after graduation to pursue further study in the U.S.A. and to secure employment there (2).

Again, the traditional educational philosophy was brought up. The purpose of education was to cultivate an ethical person, not merely a storehouse of knowledge. It seemed that the ethical purpose of education was weakened. As a matter of fact, the reasons why the students did not want to return to Taiwan were given in the above article; and the formal excuses of not finding suitable jobs and environment for doing research could not stand, for only a few graduates were qualified to give them as excuses. Concerning the parents' viewpoint, it is true that they liked their children to pursue further study and to receive higher degrees. This has been a hope all through the long history of China. However, some parents actually wanted their children to work in the U.S.A. since the incomes received there were much more than in Taiwan. In many instances, the children were forced to go abroad so that their parents' social status would be equal to that of some relatives and friends whose children had made a good living in the U.S.A.

A third article published by the Central Daily News entitled "Self-Strengthening Movement Goes On" appeared on June 1, 1975. It also concentrated criticism on the college students planning to study abroad and to stay permanently in the U.S.A. In this article, the author pointed out that the formation of the college students' thought was due to the influence of their parents who were forced to leave the China Mainland to come to Taiwan in 1949. Because of their bitter experience as refugees in Taiwan, they had influenced their children with an extremely practical attitude, such as studying hard to get into the university and putting studying as the most important thing. Furthermore, they encouraged their children to pursue advanced study abroad and to remain in the foreign country for good. The author was pitiful on those students who planned to stay in the U.S.A. or had worked in the U.S.A. for some time, and their number reached 20,000 to 30,000 people. He cited such a phenomenon as a tragedy for the Chinese intellectuals. Finally, the students were requested to wake up and to carry on the salvation of the nation (3).

The parents' attitudes are understandable. A lot of people lost their property and had to start everything again in Taiwan. Since the parents' generation had suffered so much, they surely would base their hope on the children. Also, since Taiwan is not their "real" home, moving to another country for safety makes little difference.

Besides using articles to persuade the students to return, the editor of the Central Daily News also used concrete cases as examples. On June 9, 1975, a special case was used for propaganda. In an interview by news reporters, Dr. Hua, Yih-Sun, 33 years of age, who received his doctoral degree of law from St. Louis University in Missouri and who also was an attorney in St. Louis, told the reporters that he would take up a professorship in the Graduate School of Law in the China Cultural College. In reply to the reporters' question why he gave up a well paid position as an attorney in the U.S.A. and returned to Taiwan, he stated that he wanted to use his concrete action to convince his American friends that not all Chinese students would take the United States as a paradise for permanent residence (5).

Consequences of the Movement of Nationalist Chinese Students Studying Abroad

It would be essential to examine the impacts of the large number of Chinese students staying permanently in the U.S.A. and their return to Taiwan. A large proportion of the Chinese students studying in the U.S.A. depended on financial aides, such as research assistantships or part-time work (4). Such financial aide was available to students majoring in natural sciences, engineering and fields related to medicine. U.S. industries and job market also need such specialists. Such a "brain drain" surely would hurt the development of industries, national economy, defense, education and public health in Taiwan (2). However, their return would be a great help to the national development.

The following example could be used to illustrate the impacts of the drainage of professionals from a developing country like Taiwan.

A Chinese medical student in Boston had told his friends that he would return to Taiwan by the end of June, 1975. After five years of training, that medical student became a neuropathic surgeon and also received his permanent residence visa to stay in the U.S.A. He predicted that he would have a good income and a comfortable living and political security in the U.S.A. However, he could not forget that he was a Chinese and was grateful for the education he had received in China. Because of the lack of experience in surgery, many neuropathic physicians in Taiwan could not operate on their patients and many patients lost their lives.

When that U.S.-educated student decided to return to Taiwan, nobody could believe it. Many thought it would be wise to stay in the U.S. However, he knew that it was the duty of the Chinese intellectuals to bear the responsibility of the time. Why were there so few students returning to Taiwan willingly? It was because they were too selfish and clever. What Taiwan needed today was a group of 'fools' who would work hard and make sacrifices. Although those who first returned would face a lot of hardship, pioneers were needed. To work for other people (implying the Americans) a person could not have success and would always be treated as a second class citizen (6).

In this case, the physician's return to Taiwan was a result of the calling and needs of the patients in Taiwan and patriotism and also of the negative sides of staying in the U.S.

It is fortunate that the number of students, who have completed their education in foreign countries, returning to Taiwan is increasing each year. For example, in 1962, 1,596 students went abroad for further studies and only 56 returned to Taiwan after the complettion of their education (8, pp. 521-522); in 1964, 1,417 students went abroad for further studies and only 96 returned to Taiwan, among them 55 from the U.S.A. and 21 from Japan (9, p. 475); in 1970, 407 students returned to Taiwan, among them 237 from the U.S.A., 109 from Japan, 18 from West Germany (13, p. 146). The National Youth Commission, a unit under the Executive Yuan (branch or department) of the Nationalist Government, reported that in the past four years, from 1971-1975, it has assisted 2,500 returned students to find employment in Taiwan, approximately five hundred a year. (The percentages of the returning students constituted about 25 percent of the students who went abroad for advanced studies between 1970-75). Besides, the Commission added that many returning students did not need the assistance of the Commission because they secured employment themselves or were recruited directly by certain agencies in Taiwan (7).

Summary and Discussion

Although the ideal educational policy of Nationalist China is the realization of the Three Principles of the People, nationalism, democracy and social well-being in order to prolong the life of the nation and to develop the national characteristics and traditional morality (12, p. 5), actually the policy is not so much supported by the intellectuals and their parents. More than ninety-five percent of the two thousand college graduates each year who were admitted to the graduate school for advanced studies abroad did not return to serve their country in the mid-1960's. In the early 1970's, the increased number of returning students was due to the limited employment opportunities and the limited issuance of the permanent residence visa to students in the U.S.A. (15, p. 38) and in Canada.

Although the ideal of the Nationalist Government is the return of the students to work in Taiwan, it has not actually tried to recruit them in large scale and has not taken any action to call them back. Under such a condition, some parents have encouraged their children to pursue further studies in the U.S.A. or have even forced them to go. It is a good opportunity to make a fortune. In many cases the students were forced by their parents to come to the United States and told not to return to Taiwan after the completion of their education. Thus, the parents were not supporting the educational policy of the country or helping to meet the country's needs. Such development was critical for Taiwan.

BIBLIOGRAPHY--CHAPTER IX

1. Taipei, Central Daily News, May 6, 1975.

2. _____, _____ _____ _____, May 16, 1975.

3. _____, _____ _____ _____, June 1, 1975.

4. _____, _____ _____ _____, June 8, 1975.

5. _____, _____ _____ _____, June 9, 1975.

6. _____, _____ _____ _____, June 11, 1975.

7. _____, _____ _____ _____, May 22, 1976.

8. China Yearbook Editorial Board, China Yearbook, 1962-1963, Taipei, China Publishing Co., 1963.

9. China Yearbook, 1965-1966.

10. China Yearbook, 1972-1973.

11. Interview with ten Chinese students in July, 1975.

12. Ministry of Education, Education in the Republic of China, Taipei, The Veteran Printing Press, 1970.

13. Ministry of Education, Educational Statistics of the Republic of China, 1971, Taipei, Taiwan, 1971.

14. Ministry of Education, Educational Statistics of the Republic of China, 1973. Taipei, Taiwan, 1973.

15. U. S. Immigration and Naturalization Service, U. S. Department of Justice, 1975 Annual Report: Immigration and Naturalization Service, Washington, D. C., 1975.

16. Wang, Yi-Chu, Chinese Intellectuals and the West, 1872-1949. Chapel Hill, University of North Carolina Press, 1966.

CHAPTER 10

EDUCATION AND THE FAMILY IN COMMUNIST CHINA

In this chapter, the relationship between education and the family is examined. After the Communists took over the China Mainland in 1949, they started to reform the education which has been a very useful tool for socialization. In the process of reforming education on the mainland, the Communists have to confront and challenge the Confucian educational thought which has dominated China for the past two thousand years. The educational thought of the Communists has been in contradiction to that of Confucian school.

Data for this chapter were mainly collected from the literature published by the Chinese Communists Government. Data on the educational policy of Communist China were collected from four articles published in two periodicals (4, 5, 7, 8) and from one article from a newspaper both of which sources have been the official organs of the Communist Government (9). Since only the official organs of the Communist Government can publish the educational policy of the nation, they have been the only source. The Communists have made use of those articles to publish cases in which their educational policy has been supported and followed by many people (7, 9).

However, there were articles, published in the same periodicals and newspapers, which carried conflicting reports and evidences, telling that the educational policy has not been supported and accepted by some people. Two of such articles were used. One was published in a periodical (6) and another in a newspaper (1), both of them official organs of the Communist Government. From the U.S.A., an article published in a professional journal (10) and a book (12) published by a recognized university press were included for the data on the actual structure between education and the family. Also included were a public document published by the Hong Kong Government (2) and interviews, by the present writer, of two individuals (3), one being a former Red Guard in Canton and the other having visited the mainland for a month in December 1975.

Two explanations could be used to explain the difference in the data. The first would be that certain people have still followed the traditional educational thought in contradiction to the educational thought of the Communists. The second explanation would be that certain aspects of the Communist educational thought have been in contradiction to the traditional Chinese culture, namely, that people prefer to be better off rather than worse off materially.

After the Communists took over the China Mainland in 1949, they started to reform in three steps the education system which existed. The first step was that the Communists demanded that the intellectuals from bourgeois family backgrounds change their attitudes and political consciousness by accepting the Communist ideology. The next step was

to replace the old intellectuals from the bourgeois class family by selecting students from the proletarian family background. The third
step was the proletarization of the intellectuals by making them live
and work with the proletariat, such as the peasants.

In this chapter, the interaction between the family and education
is examined in terms of The Proletarization of the Intellectuals from
Bourgeois Families, Changes in Educational Policy after the Cultural
Revolution, and The Proletarization of the Intellectuals by Sending
Them to the Countryside (after the early 1960's).

The Proletarization of the Intellectuals from Bourgeois Families, and Changes in Educational Policy after the Cultural Revolution

When the Communists took over the China Mainland in 1949, the intellectuals who had established their professional service in the mainland had come from the bourgeois family background. The Communists
left this group of intellectuals intact because they were needed for
the maintenance and construction of industry, education, science and
technology (4, p. 19), even though they had been brought up in bourgeois families and possessed the thinking of the bourgeoisie. Their
families of orientation included the strata of upper and upper-middle
classes, landlords, owners of business and industry, and professionals.

The Communists were also aware of the influence and impact on
those intellectuals from their family of orientation and their parents.
When the Communists tried to win over the intellectuals to their side,
the parents of those capitalist intellectuals also wanted to win over
their children to their side to make them perpetuators of capitalism.
They diffused the individual thinking of the capitalist class and
taught their children that knowledge could not be confiscated, that
technique was the most reliable capital, and that good reputation, high
position, and abundant money could be obtained by real ability. They
hoped that their children could become a special and elite class, rising above the working people (4, p. 19).

The Communists were much afraid that this group of capitalist intellectuals would take knowledge and technique as their private capital
and trade this capital for their reputation, position, and treatment
from the Communist Party. When they could not fulfill their desire,
they would cause trouble or even oppose the party and the leadership.
Besides, they might use their position to implement the ideological
lines of the capitalist class and they might eventually become the
basis for the restoration of capitalism and revisionism (4, p. 19).

Because the Communists wanted to win over the intellectuals from
exploiting families to their side, they required those intellectuals to
do several things. First, one should clearly recognize the inherent
nature of the exploitation practiced by the capitalist families and
should be aware of the crimes of exploitation committed by his own family. He should support the transformation of the capitalist families.
Secondly, one should recognize the influence of capitalist families on
oneself and should make an effort to protect oneself against the bad
influence on one's political attitude, thinking and feeling, and way of
life. Thirdly, one should have the determination to become a worker
with socialist awareness and culture and to unite with workers and

peasants (4, p. 21).

What the Communists want are intellectuals from the proletariat. Since the ideology and class line are so important to the Communists, a person's political thought is as important or even more important than his skill and work ability (4). Therefore, the Communists eventually replaced the intellectuals from capitalist families, after the Cultural Revolution, by selecting university students from among the working class.

It was in the Cultural Revolution that the educational policy of the nation demanded a drastic and complete change which would foster a group of intellectuals who would come from the proletariat and be for the proletariat. After the Cultural Revolution in 1967, the Communists changed admission policy for universities. The method of choosing students from among workers, peasants, and soldiers includes voluntary application, by the students, to one's working unit, the recommendation by the masses of people, approval by the leadership of the Party, and finally examination by the university authorities. The purpose of the new method of enrollment is to foster successors to the cause of the proletarian revolution and to bring up a force of intellectuals of the working class (9). Such a change will have considerable impact on the relationship between education and the family.

After the Communists had adopted the new education policy, they actually wanted it to be carried out as proclaimed. Although the new education policy had prevented students from bourgeois family background from entering the university, it was not fully adhered to by some high-ranking government officials themselves. Some high-ranking officials tried to use their position and influence in the Party to put their children into the university without following and going through proper channels. Since no one could accumulate great wealth in Communist China, education thus has become a value and a valuable asset to be pursued by the people.

In January 1974, a true story was published on the front page of the People's Daily, the most popular and important newspaper and official organ in Communist China. The same article, titled "An Application to Withdraw from University," was later published in Peking Review, a weekly journal published in several foreign languages. The story described the son of a high-ranking government official who was admitted into the university by the influence of his father, who later was made aware of his wrong doing, and who requested permission to withdraw from the university. The main theme of the story emphasizes the danger of the formation of an elite class and the embourgeoisement of the proletariat. The story is very interesting and contains the techniques of socialization and propaganda the Communists used.

The story began with Chih-Min Chung, the son of a high ranking official in the army. Chih-Min Chung was a second-year student in the political science department of Nanking University, and he submitted an application to his university's Party committee to give up his studies and to go back to the village, because he had gotten into the university not by the regular way, but "by the back door." His father, the holder of a responsible position, had pulled strings to get the youth admitted. His father, Chung Hsueh-Lin, a veteran in the Red Army, was on the 25,000 li Long March (the great escape in 1935 when the Chinese

Communists were chased by the Nationalist Army to the northwestern part of China) and holds an important position in a political department in the People's Liberation Army. His mother was also a veteran cadre member and is now retired.

The story began in 1968 when Chung finished junior middle school and was sent to settle in Juichin County, Kiangsi province. In the beginning, he did not want to go, but finally he went, although against his will. He had been influenced by the revisionist line in education and the ideas of Confucius and Mencius: "those who labor with their minds govern; those who labor with their physical strength are governed." However, his parents agreed to get him out of the village as soon as opportunity came. A year later he went to see a responsible member in the county department of the armed forces and pleaded that "special considerations" be granted to him to join the People's Liberation Army. He was accepted into the army because of his parents' position. Then, he wanted to go to the university. Telling himself that a bit of "prerogative" in his case was in order, he asked his parents to see if they could use their influence to help him because he was the son of the revolutionary parents with "meritorious record." His father then talked to the department personnel concerned, and Chung was accepted into the University. Since he did not have the recommendations from his army unit to go to the university, his action did not win approval from comrades-in-arms. When he arrived in the university, he wished to write a letter to his unit expressing his determination not to disappoint the Party organization's hope in him, but he did not have the courage to do so (6, p. 11).

In more than a year of studying the works of Marx, Lenin, and Mao Tse-Tung, of working in the factories, mines, and farms, and of taking part in revolution and production and being re-educated by workers and poor peasants, Chung's political consciousness began to improve. By close contact with the workers and peasants, he found out that they were strongly against doing things "by the back door," and he felt sorry for what he had done.

In the summer vacation of 1973, he spent three days with an uncle living in Juichin County. While talking with his cousins on family matters, he learned that his paternal grandfather and other revolutionaries had organized and taken part in an armed uprising against the exploiting classes in 1929. After the Red Army withdrew from their village, his grandfather was arrested and murdered by Kuomintang (Nationalist Party) reactionaries. The grandmother decided to send her three sons to join the Red Army. One of his uncles was caught and beaten to death by landlords after he was severely wounded during the Long March. Another uncle lost his life during the Long March. The revolutionary family's history gave him a profound class education. He thought that if the descendants of the revolutionaries only relied on the meritorious record of their parents, it was very dangerous because they were not following their parents' footsteps. He decided to leave the university.

Having returned from his holidays, on September 28, 1973, Chung wrote an application to the university Party committee to withdraw from the university by saying

"Going in by the back door" involves the question of whom

122

are we to serve. Chairman Mao has said: "All our cadres, whatever their rank, are servants of the people, and whatever we do is to serve the people." The practice of "going in by the back door" actually means abusing the power granted by the people to further one's own selfish ends. This is an expression of bourgeois ideology of benefiting oneself at the expense of others, comes from the decadent class and is diametrically opposed to the interests of the majority of the people (6, p. 11).

In his criticism of "going in by the back door" Chung said in his application report:

When some cadres get their children into college "by the back door" without first getting the recommendation and nomination of the masses and approval of the local leadership but only on the authority of their position and personal relations it prevents really fine workers, peasants and soldiers from entering. This hurts the Party's relations with the broad masses of people and damages the fine tradition of the Party and is fundamentally contrary to the proletarian Party spirit.
     If cadres' children enjoy "special consideration," Chung Chih-Min added, "a privileged stratum" could easily emerge and their children could very easily become revisionists. The great revolutionary teachers have all repeatedly warned of the possibility of this happening. Soviet social-imperialist reality and the practice of the Great Proletarian Cultural Revolution clearly show that if children of those cadres who enjoy rather better living conditions are divorced for a long time from the worker-peasant masses and from productive world outlook they can fall easy prey to bourgeois ideology and become revisionists. This is very dangerous! Is this lovely land of our parents and other revolutionary forebears won through so much sacrifice to come to an end with us? No! Never! We must not be dependent on our parents. Politically, we must continue the cause they have pursued and carry on the proletarian revolution they have not finished through to the end (6, p. 12)

Of course, the parents later also understood that they had made a mistake and that their actions stemmed from bourgeois ideology. They were enlightened by Mao's teachings concerning the bringing up of millions of successors to the proletariat and about how the educated young people responded to the call to go to the countryside to be integrated with workers and peasants. The father realized that as a senior leading cadre of the Party he should set a good example for the people. The parents sent a telegram to Nanking University Party committee to support their son's application to withdraw from the university and a self criticism. In the telegram, they said, "Our son belongs to the Party, he should comply with arrangements made for him by the Party. We are determined to let our son steel himself and grow up in the three great revolutionary movements to become a reliable and worthy successor to the revolutionary cause of the proletariat." (6, p. 19)

This article, combined with other publications about Communist ideology, invite several speculations.

It suggests that a large number of the educated youths do not like to be sent to the countryside as life there is hard and poor. The present writer was told by a youth who left Communist China to come to Hong Kong that many young people in the countryside were always wanting to come to the city because it is superior to the countryside in many ways, such as in social and cultural activities, and in material supplies (3). Such a desire is common in U.S. history and is present, also, in other countries that have moved or that are moving to modernization.

Further, education is still a value which carries rewards of prestige and status. While the children of the proletariat were not able to be admitted into the university before the Communist regime was established, the parents in the proletariat want their children to go there now. The method of admission by recommendation rather than only by economic capability and prestige status has encouraged the parents to urge their children toward getting more education.

Also, although the youth are educated by the Party and in political education outside the family, it is evident that some of the ideas and thoughts, which are contrary to the Communist ideology, very possibly are learned in the family.

Also, some families apparently still give assistance to the children in their choice of education and career, such as was given in the case of Chung Chih-Min. It could be a "common" practice in Communist China for the high-ranking cadres to use their influence to put their children into the university or 'good jobs.' It is quite evident that the senior and high-ranking cadres unnoticeably could have become an 'elite' stratum as they were the founders of the People's Republic. It is natural for them to collect their fair share now. Otherwise this article very probably needed not to be put on the front page of the People's Daily, the most important and representative newspaper in the nation.

In the above story, one can see that the Communists have relied heavily on the educational and social approaches to transform the people, at least as the affair can be seen from the story, and especially since education is expected to relate constructively to social change.

The Proletarization of the Intellectuals by Sending Them to the
Countryside beginning from the early 1960's

Since the early 1960's, the Communists have been sending millions of high school and college graduates to the countryside to live and work with the peasants. Truly it is against the cultural values of the traditional society which upholds mental labor and looks down on physical labor. Besides, agriculture is not a "respectable" career in the mind of the intellectuals. Perhaps the real reason for sending the youths to the countryside is the lack of suitable job opportunities in the city and a way to solve the population problem. However, it may be a method to modernize the rural areas by providing professional service and initiating new ideas to the rural population (5, pp. 12-14; 7, pp. 19-21, 31). It would also, of course, help prevent a cultural rift between "intellectuals" and "the people."

In order to make the educated youths (mostly secondary school graduates) to go to the countryside willingly, the Communists have used a lot of efforts to explain, persuade, comfort and encourage them to go. A speech by Wang Jen-Ch'ung clearly implies what are the reflections of the youths who are going to be sent to the countryside. Wang was the Second Secretary of the Central-South Bureau, Chinese Communist Party Central Committee, December 1961-September 1966; and the Political Commissar of the People's Liberation Army, Wuhan Military Region, March 1963-1967 (11, p. 678). In his lengthy speech, Wang stated that it was the purpose of the Communist Party to build a socialist new rural village which would be composed of a new type of peasant with a high degree of socialist awareness and scientific knowledge. Since eighty percent of the national population lived in the countryside and the rural village was very poor and backward, it would be necessary to improve the rural area for socialist construction.

To be a peasant was also to be a revolutionary warrior because the Party designed the rural countryside as the first front line of a struggle and the educated youths were mostly needed there. The peasants were revolutionary warriors because they joined the liberation army and participated in the liberation war, fighting against the class enemies, natural catastrophes, traditional customs and superstitions such as arranging and purchasing of marriages, and against the dominance of the clans. Although life would be hard and difficult, said Wang, improvement and progress in the rural areas would have to depend on the hard work of the educated youths. They would be the channel for spreading new thoughts, culture and techniques, but only after first being integrated with the peasants. They would have to create cultural, recreational, and political activities, and also educational extensions. To bring communism into realization, the Communists must eliminate distinctions between city and the rural country, workers and peasants, mental labor and manual labor. The new socialist countryside has been under construction and was improving, according to Wang. In the future, rural areas would be mechanized and the distinction between workers and peasants would be eliminated. The educated youths engaged in farming and cultural activities and were considered to be both mental and manual laborers.

The individual future of the educated youths was equivalent to the future of the new socialistic countryside which was linked to the future of the nation. In the future, many of them would become cadres, scientists, writers and scientists through independent study. Since there was a limited number of vacancies in the university, the majority of secondary school graduates would have to go to work. They might surpass the college students through independent study. The party was the instructor; and the revolution and labor were the university for the youths (1).

From the above discussion, a person could see that the Communists have nowhere to put these educated youths but the rural countryside. However, the problem has not been solved that easily. The present writer interviewed a former Red Guard in Hong Kong in October 1972 who had been sent to the countryside for farming. He came to Hong Kong in early 1972 and revealed that most of the educated youths were against being sent to the countryside, because they understood that only the

125

bad elements were sent there. The peasants did not welcome them because the educated youths did not know any farming but nevertheless shared the food. Also, the students were unhappy because there were not enough suitable jobs assigned to them in the city. After the Cultural Revolution the industrial workers were badly needed to rebuild the national economy and they were most honored and respected and could enjoy special privileges. Most of the former Red Guards became very frustrated because they felt that they had been used in the Cultural Revolution; and then they were dropped into the countryside afterwards. Since they were told to learn from the poor peasant about the revolution and class struggle, such a trend would only lower the educational level of the educated youths (3).

The present writer also interviewed another informant, his close relative, who visited his family in the mainland in December, 1975. In Canton he visited the aunt of the present writer and was told that the two nieces of the present writer were sent to the countryside around Canton after graduation from high school. The older niece, being brighter, was working in a drug factory in a town nearby and could come home every week. The younger one was working in a far distant farm and could return home only once a month. Most of the high school graduates, as in the case of Canton, were sent to the countryside for two years and those who showed good performance in political ideology and participation and in their assigned work would be selected to go to university for further professional training (3).

There were millions of high school graduates sent to the countryside to do farm work. Such a migration of the educated youths to the rural areas might have considerable impacts on the family of these youths from the city. In the first place, the family influence and control on these youths would be reduced and on the contrary Party education and political group pressures and associations would increase as these youths would be placed under the supervisions and instructions of the political cadres (8, p. 14). The Communists hoped that the traditional cultural values possessed by these youths could be eliminated, such as the concern for individual future and career (1).

The Communists have tried to indoctrinate these youths that the future of the nation was equivalent to the future of the individual and that the interests of the individual must be submitted to the interests of the nation (1). Secondly, the Communists hoped that these youths could bring some changes on the traditions and customs on the rural areas (1). For example, the Marriage Law promulgated by the Central Government in 1950, could only reach fifteen percent of the population in the nation on those living in cities and towns and it was ignored in rural areas (12, p. 140). Besides, a researcher reported that in rural areas, the parents are still in control of the children on their education and work (10, p. 715). Therefore, the Communists really needed to change the political and ideological thinking of the people in the countryside in order that the Central Government can exercise control over the population in the nation as a whole.

Summary and Discussion

Ideally speaking, the Communists expect to have a group of proletarian intellectuals to provide professional services to the industry, commerce, agriculture and education in the nation. However, this ideal could not be realized at least in the first two decades after the establishment of their regime. The problem to cultivate the proletarian intellectuals is still a problem even in the 1970's.

After the Communists took over the China Mainland in 1949, they did not find the proletarian intellectuals they wanted. So, they had to make use of those intellectuals who had already established their professional service there before 1949. In reality, the Communists had to depend on a group of intellectuals from the bourgeois family background. The Communists could not fully trust this group of intellectuals and demanded them to change their political ideology which might be in contradiction to their family heritage. On the other hand, the parents of these intellectuals just did the opposite socialization to those of the Communists. Eventually, the Communists decided gradually to replace this group of intellectuals from the bourgeois family background in the Cultural Revolution in the mid-1960's.

One method to replace the intellectuals from the bourgeois family background was to admit students to the university only from the proletarian family background. This ideal admission policy was actually practiced during and after the Cultural Revolution to shut off students from bourgeois family background from admission. However, this ideal admission policy was not honored by some high ranking Communist officials who had used their influence to put their children into the university without following the new admission policy. The Central (national) Government was aware of such a practice and warned its officials not to use their influence to put their children in the university.

The second area in which education and the family are related is the sending of the high school and college graduates from the city to the countryside. Ideally the Communists expected that the youths would be willingly sent to the countryside and stay there with the peasants by obeying the order of the Party and the Central Government. Actually, the situation was not that smooth. As reflected from Wang's speech (1), Wang had to persuade and explain to the youths that they had to sacrifice themselves and their personal career in order to become pioneers in the agricultural frontier and to create a new socialist countryside. Wang also tried to convince the youths that they could study by themselves and by correspondence courses even though they were not admitted into the university. However, after the Cultural Revolution, some of the youths sent to the countryside would be selected to go to the university if their political participation and work performance were outstanding (6, p. 11).

In reality, many youths were reluctant to be sent to the countryside or could not stand the hardship there. A considerable number of them escaped to Hong Kong through the border or by sea. Such a problem caused some concern to the Hong Kong Government as "illegal immigration continued to cause concern, with 17,271 detected as having entered illegally during the year (1972), an increase of 0.37 percent of the preceeding year. The main source of illegal entry are China, Maucau and the countries of South-East Asia." (2, p. 121)

1. Peking, Chinese Youth Daily, Chung-kuo Ching-nien Pao, May 28, 1964.

2. Hong Kong Government, Hong Kong 1973, A Review of 1972, Hong Kong Government Press, 1973.

3. Interview with a former Red Guard in Hong Kong in October 1972 and another informant in January 1976.

4. Liu, Ching-Nung, "The Bright Future of Youths from Capitalist Families," Chinese Youth, (September 1, 1964), 18-21.

5. Pai, Chi-Hsin, "Integration with the Poor and Lower-Middle Peasants," Peking Review, (July 26, 1974), 12-14.

6. "An Application to Withdraw from University," Peking Review, (February 22, 1974), 10-12, 19.

7. "Taking the Revolutionary Path of Going to the Countryside," Peking Review, (May 10, 1974), 19-21, 31.

8. "A Good Way to Settle Educated Youth in the Countryside," Peking Review (August 2, 1974), 13-15.

9. Peking, People's Daily, Jen-min Jih-pao, March 4, 1972.

10. Salaff, Janet W., "The Emerging Conjugal Relationship in the People's Republic of China," Journal of Marriage and the Family, (November, 1973), 705-717.

11. Union Research Institute, Who's Who in Communist China, Hong Kong, Union Press, 1970.

12. Walker, Richard L., China Under Communism, New Haven, Yale University Press, 1955; in Lucy Jen Huang, "Some Changing Patterns in Communist Chinese Family," Marriage and Family Living (May, 1961), 137-146.

CHAPTER 11

SUMMARY AND CONCLUSIONS

Chapter XI is a chapter of summary and conclusions and contains the findings from the study and discussion, future trends of the family in Nationalist China and Communist China, and recommendations for further studies.

In section two, data collected on the future trends of the family in Nationalist China and Communist China included mainly public documents. For the family in Nationalist China, data were collected from five documents (11-14) and eight articles (2-9) of a newspaper which are official organs of the Nationalist Government which alone can provide demographic statistics and express the official opinions of the Nationalist government. No conflicting evidences were found among the data indicating the trends of industrialization and urbanization in Taiwan.

For the family in Communist China, sixteen articles (16-21, 23-31, 36) were collected from a periodical which is an official organ of the Communist Government. Since only an official organ can publish the policy and priorities of the Communist Government, it is the only source available to obtain data of such a nature. No conflicting evidences were found, of course.

Summary and Discussion

In this section, the summary of the findings of this study was given and would be followed by discussion.

Introduction to the Study

The purpose of this study was to examine the changes in the age and sex hierarchies in the family in Nationalist China on Taiwan and in Communist China on the China Mainland from the traditional family. The age and sex hierarchies have been the most basic support of the traditional family. The relationship and interaction between education and the family were also examined.

Changes in the Age Hierarchy in the Chinese Family

In chapter one, questions were raised on the changes of the age hierarchy: What were the changes in the family power structures in terms of age of its members, with respect to the following, relative to the family in traditional China: a) control of family finance, b) decisions about other important family affairs, such as divisions and inheritance of family property, choice of career and profession, d) de-

cisions about the education of the children, e) socializing and upholding the values and ideals of the family members, f) control of the ideology of the family members, g) younger generation's attitude toward
power in the family?

The Age Hierarchy in the Family in Traditional China

The dominance of the age hierarchy (the dominance of the patriarchal system) was a significant feature in the traditional Chinese family.
The patriarch was the legal representative of the family in paying
taxes and rents, the legal guardian of family property and the conduct
of the members of his family of procreation, arranged the marriage of
his children, their education and occupation (mainly for the male members).

The ideal and the actual family structures in the traditional China were closely identical because the "law of clan organization," by
Duke Chou, and the Five Cardinal Relations, by Confucius, were supported and put into practice by the rulers in traditional China. The rulers
realized that the ideal family structure modeled by Confucius was very
useful to cultivate faithful and obedient children in the family and
citizens in the nation. Besides, it would be easy to control the country, such as through the patriarchal system and the father-son relationship.

The Age Hierarchy in the Family in Republic China

The dominance of the older generation over the younger generations
was challenged in the Republican Period, especially in the May Fourth
Movement in 1919. The traditional family was criticized as being the
center of loyalty, and the interests of the family were put above those
of the country and the individual members. The ruling of the older
generation in society and in the family was challenged and charged as
a hindrance to the progress and the sacrifice of individual career.

The challenge and criticism of the age hierarchy were due to the
influence of western ideas, such as equality and freedom, and industrialization and urbanization, and several young intellectuals and
scholars led the challenges and attacks on the age hierarchy in the
family as well as in society. After the Chinese Republic was established in 1912, the traditional, imperial laws were abolished. A Civil
Code was promulgated in 1930 which preserved much of the authority of
the patriarch. However, the Civil Code was ahead of its time and was
not enforced.

The Changes in the Age Hierarchy in the Family
in Nationalist China

The age hierarchy in Nationalist China on Taiwan was the perpetuation of the age hierarchy from the Republican Period. The ethical
teachings of Confucius, such as the Five Cardinal Relations, have been
upheld as the ideal normative pattern in many families. The patriarchal system still exists but the patriarch does not have the absolute
power to control the livelihood of the grown-up children; however, the

patriarch is still responsible for the conduct of the minors in his family of procreation. In the family of orientation of the intellectuals (college students), not always does the patriarch control the family finance, education and marriage of the children and even the important decisions in the family affairs. But, many patriarchs of the lower strata and in rural areas still try to arrange the marriage of their children, and some have met with resistance.

Although the Confucian ethics of the Cardinal Relations has been upheld as the ideal for kinship relations, by some high-ranking officials and scholars in Nationalist China, the Nationalist Government has not enforced any normative patterns of kinship relations or imposed any regulations on the people. The Government leaves a free hand to the people and lets the individual and their families work out their patterns of kinship relations. So, various forms of family structures can be observed in Taiwan. A person may observe conservatism among the older generation and liberalism among the young. For the long run, the trend may move towards the direction of the mixture of the Chinese and western family structure. The Civil Code of 1930 is still the law of kinship relations in Taiwan.

The Changes of the Age Hierarchy in the Family in Communist China

The age hierarchy in Communist China has been challenged by the Communists since 1949, following the establishment of their regime on the China Mainland. With the abolition of the patriarchal system, the Communists launched ideological attacks on filial piety for the purpose of weakening the links between the parents and the children, hoping the younger generations would put the interests of the state, not the parents', in first place. The decisions on the future career and the pursuit of higher education have been increasingly controlled by the government, being taken from the family. After the promulgation of the Marriage Law in 1950, the Communists have made special efforts to prevent the parents from interfering with the children's marriage. However, in actuality, it appears that the parents still have considerable influence on the children's marriage, and/or on the pursuit of education or work in the rural areas. The parents are still in control of the family finance and other affairs in the rural villages. Therefore, the ideal and the actual family structures have not coincided in the rural areas.

One of the reasons for the Communists to change the family on the China Mainland was to replace the family by the state as the center of loyalty and allegiance for the people, especially the younger generations. Therefore, the patriarchal system was first abolished so that the head of the family could no longer control the younger generations. Besides, ideally speaking, since the family can no longer possess the means of production, the family can no longer control the livelihood of its members. Also, the government has taken over the control of education and employment in the nation. Filial piety was the most important link between the parents and the children in the traditional family. The Communists have tried to weaken and replace filial piety in the family by the appeal of patriotism and nationalism. Familism dominated the traditional family and society and is not considered suitable for the development of an industrial society.

Changes in the Sex Hierarchy in the Chinese Family

In chapter one, questions were raised on the changes in the sex hierarchy in the Chinese family: What were the changes in the sex hierarchy in the family with respect to the following for the females: a) the status of the female members in the family, b) the opportunity to receive formal education and secure gainful employment outside the family, c) the freedom of marriage, divorce, and re-marriage, d) freedom to participate in social and political activities?

The Sex Hierarchy in the Family in Traditional China

The dominance of the sex hierarchy (the emphasis on the father-son relationship) began after the establishment of the "law of clan organization" by Duke Chou and later the elaboration of Confucius. In the clan and family, line of descent must be patrilineal; it was father-right in which the status, office, privileges, property, etc. would be passed from the father to the sons. It was patriarchal and primogeniture. The dominance of men over women of the same generation and of later generations was a unique characteristic in the family and in society. Discriminations against women included the deprivation of the opportunities to receive formal education, professional training, and gainful employment because men played most of the important roles in society.

In the traditional family, the ideal structure of the sex hierarchy, based on the "law of clan organization" by Duke Chou and the ethical teachings of the Five Cardinal Relations by Confucius, was supported by the ruler in traditional China. Therefore, the "law of clan organization" was adopted as law and the traditional family was thus patrilineal, patriarchal and patrilocal. Since men took over the main duty of economic production in the agrarian society, women became their dependents and occupied a subordinate position.

The Sex Hierarchy in the Family in Republican China

The dominance of the sex hierarchy, the dominance of men over women, was challenged in the Republican Period. The subordinate, low status of women in society and in the family was thus challenged. Equal opportunity to receive education, employment, property rights, freedom to choose marriage partners, divorce and re-marriage and freedom to participate in social and political activities were demanded. As a result of the challenge to the sex hierarchy, the Civil Code of 1930 was promulgated as a new family law of China. However, in the Code, considerable favorable treatments were given to the male members in the family. The Civil Code was actually ahead of its time and was not enforced.

The challenge to the sex hierarchy was due to the influence of western culture, such as in the latter's individual freedom and equality. The challenge was led by some intellectuals who saw the injustice and unfairness in the treatment of women in society and in the family. They believed those had hindered the progress of the nation.

132

The Changes in the Sex Hierarchy in the Family in Nationalist China

The sex hierarchy in the family in Nationalist China has been the perpetuation of the changes in Republican China. While the traditional family structure and the Confucian ethics still have considerable influence in Taiwan, it is certain that the dominance of men over women still exists. Although the Civil Code of 1930 is the family law of Nationalist China which already gives considerable favorable treatments to men, a law authority observed that the inequality of women in relation to men in the family was much worse than in the regulations in the Civil Code of 1930. Statistical records of school enrollments showed that the ratio of boys to girls was three to two. Also, women have few leadership roles in politics, and it appears that half of the women drop out of work after marriage. Freedom of marriage, divorce and remarriage was kept from the female members in the peasant, working class families.

Although the ideal of sex equality is written in the Constitution and supported by the Nationalist Government, yet the ideal has not been realized. In reality, the actual family structure is still based on the traditional kinship relations, and the dominance of men over women still exists, especially among the peasant and working class families. As a matter of fact, the Nationalist Government has not taken any action to enforce the ideal of sex equality in the areas of education, employment, and marriage among the lower strata.

The Changes in the Sex Hierarchy in the Family in Communist China

In Communist China, the sex hierarchy has been a target for the Communists. The promulgation of the Marriage Law in 1950 gives equality and protection to women in marriage, family living, divorce and remarriage. New concepts concerning marriage, such as the new wedding ceremony and customs, sex equality in family living, etc., brought some new insights for sex equality. Divorce became a problem to the Communists a few years after the promulgation of the Marriage Law because the young married couples were thrown into a period of anomie. Women's participation in economic production and political activities has been encouraged by the Communists because they are essential for women's independence. Therefore, a large percentage of women have participated in economic production, and a considerable number of women have been elected to political offices. Although the Communist Government has tried very hard to bring sex equality into actuality, the Communists also have admitted that they have not yet fully achieved their goals. The traditions from the past two thousand years could not be eliminated in a short time, especially in rural areas.

The ideal of sex equality advocated by the Communists has been a mechanism to break away from the control of women by men in the family, namely, half of the population in the nation. The Communists want the allegiance and loyalty of all the people to the Communist Party and the state. Participation of women in economic production and political activities have been encouraged and demanded by the Communists as the two prerequisites for women's independence. Of course, women's labor force is needed by the Communists for the national economy.

133

Education and the Family in China

One purpose of this study was to identify the relationship and interaction between education and the family in traditional, Republican, Nationalist and Communist China.

Education and the Family in Traditional China

In traditional China, the educational thought of the Confucian school dominated China for the past two thousand years. The Confucian educational thought included ethics and morality and the aims of education were to cultivate a moral and ethical person so that he could manage his family and country well. Education also produced two social classes--the educated ruled over the uneducated, namely, those who used the brain should rule over those who used their hands. Rulers in traditional China established the civil service examinations and the candidates who passed the examinations would serve as officials in the government and would be rewarded with wealth, power and prestige. Because of those rewards, the parents in the traditional family strongly and earnestly supported education and urged their sons to study and prepare to take the civil service examinations. The families of the wealthy and of officials were in a much better position to prepare their sons to take and pass the examinations and to perpetuate their family status. Thus, the ideal educational policy became an actuality.

In traditional China, education and the family had a very close relationship as the educational thought of the Confucian school was supported by the family and used by the rulers to control the intellectuals and rule the country. Because Confucius strongly emphasized the importance of education for the cultivation of a moral person, the parents would welcome such a teaching for the cultivation of filial sons and obedient citizens. Besides, the civil service examinations were strongly supported by the parents because the successful candidates would bring wealth, prestige and power to the family and the parents would be honored by the son's success. Also, the family background had much to do with the candidate's success because the family provided the education, and sometimes illegitimate methods were used by the family to help the candidates to pass the examinations. Therefore, the families of the wealthy and officials could perpetuate their family status through education.

Education and the Family in Republican China

In the Republican Period, the educational thought of the Confucian school was under criticism and attacks. It was charged with being too conservative and too unable to meet the needs of the time. At the same time, science and technology continued being introduced to the Chinese intellectuals and gradually gained acceptance in educational institutions. When the educational institutions were gradually absorbing the western culture, the opportunities to receive an education were still the privileges of the few--the wealthy families. Higher education was still monopolized by the rich families, including the opportunities to pursue further studies abroad. A considerable number of students, who had received westernized education, lived in the cities and pursued their professional careers outside the civil service. Thus, the modern intellectuals did not play the role as the intermediaries between the people and the local government as their counterparts in traditional China.

The ideal of educational policy in the Republican Period was the realization of the Three Principles of the People--nationalism, democracy and social well-being--by Dr. Sun Yat-Sen. Although the intellectuals in the Republican Period did not control the political power as had their counterparts in traditional China, they were very patriotic if judged by their participation in the May Fourth Movement and in fighting against the Japanese invasion during World War II. However, democracy and social well-being, the other two principles, were not realized. At least they were not realized by the intellectuals.

Education and the Family in Nationalist China

In Nationalist China, there existed a conflict of interests between the family, students, and the educational policy of the nation. The ideal of the educational policy of Nationalist China is the realization of the Three Principles of the People, and the cultivation of moral characters of the students. Unfortunately, there existed a phenomenon unusual to the Chinese intellectuals in the 1960's. A large number of the most qualified, needed college graduates and professionals left the country for further studies and stayed in the U.S.A., and later in Canada, in the early 1970's. They did so for various reasons, including finding suitable environments for further research and for performance of their highly professional knowledge and skills. The majority could find better job opportunities and rewards there than in Taiwan.

The problem of a large number of college graduates staying permanently in other countries might be due to the problem of the over-production of college graduates. Up to the mid-1960's, the industry and economy in Taiwan were still underdeveloped; at the same time, it faced a problem of the over-production of college graduates. Thus, the Nationalist Government did not interfere with the migration of her students. The attraction of material welfare and a good income influenced the large majority to stay in foreign countries. Thus, in actuality, the ideal of the educational policy of Nationalist China--The Three Principles of the People--has not been fulfilled, without the support of the students and their family.

Actually, the problem on the return of the highly trained college graduates touches on the problem of the developing countries and the over-production of college graduates and professionals. Usually, the developing countries have a problem of population explosion and the underdevelopment of economy and industry. Therefore, the over-production of intellectuals could create a problem of suitable employment in those countries. However, professionals in the fields of sciences, engineering, technology and health sciences are badly needed in the developing countries and it is the same group that the highly industrialized countries also want. So, the highly industrialized countries should also bear the responsibilities for the "brain drain" of the professionals from the developing countries. Taiwan, as one of the developing countries, has also faced the problem of the over-production of intellectuals and professionals and the underdevelopment of industry and economy.

Education and the Family in Communist China

In Communist China, when the Chinese Communists took over the China Mainland in 1949, it was the victory of the proletariat over the bourgeoisie. Ideally speaking, the Communists expected and would like to see a group of proletarian intellectuals to take charge of the professional services in the country. But in actuality, the Communists only found a group of bourgeois intellectuals who had already established their professional services in the China Mainland. Since the Communists had to depend on the professional services of the intellectuals from the bourgeois family, the former left the groups intact. However, the Communists still required those intellectuals from the bourgeois family to change their political thought and viewpoints to those of the proletariat. But, at the same time, the parents of those intellectuals kept on socializing their children with the thinking of the bourgeoisie and thus were in conflict with the plan of the Communists.

When the Communists had no other choice but to depend on the professional services of the bourgeois intellectuals in the first two decades of their rule, they still could not fully trust the latter. The Communists decided to gradually replace the intellectuals from the bourgeois family by those from the proletarian family background. Thus, after the Cultural Revolution in 1967, the Communists decided to admit students into the university only from the proletarian family background with outstanding records of political thinking, participations, and work performance. Ideally such an admission policy could gradually produce the intellectuals of and for the proletariat. But, unfortunately, in actuality some high-ranking government officials tried to use their position and influence to put their children, who did not meet the requirements of the new admission policy, into the university. Therefore, the Central Government in Peking warned the officials to honor the new admission policy, since family prestige and/or privilege position were not to be used instead of political and/or academic qualifications of the individual applicant.

After the middle of the 1960's, large numbers of high school and college graduates were sent to the countryside to live and work with the peasants. The Communists expected the youths would, ideally, accept their work allocation willingly as the proletarian intellectuals should. But, in actuality, it seems many of the youths have been reluctant to go to the countryside to engage in farming. The Communists attributed this to family's contamination of the thought of those youths. By sending the youths to the countryside, the Communists would lessen the influence of the family on those youths, and at the same time political indoctrination by the Communists would increase.

During the Cultural Revolution, the demand for intellectuals of and for the proletariat developed. The method to achieve such a goal was to admit into the university those students from the proletarian family background, with outstanding political and work performance.

Since the mid-1960's, millions of high school and college graduates from the cities were sent to the countryside to live and work with the peasants. The Communists stated that such a movement was for the proletarization of the intellectuals by living with the peasants and workers; and to build a new socialist countryside. However, the real reason might be that there were not enough jobs suitable for the youths in the city. Besides, since the large majority of the high school graduates could not enter the university due to limited vacancies, the only alternative was to put them to work.

The Future Trends of the Family in Nationalist China

The future trends of the family in Nationalist China may be towards the ideal family structure in the Civil Code if the following favorable conditions materialize, namely, industrialization, urbanization, and the continuous influence of the western culture. These three areas are closely related, since industrialization will lead to urbanization which will help lead to the acceptance of the western culture.

Industrialization in Nationalist China

The development of industrialization in Nationalist China during the past fifteen years can be seen in the occupation distributions of population in 1960 (11, pp. 122-123), 1970 (12, p. 106) and 1975 (14, p. 133).

TABLE I

POPULATION DISTRIBUTION BY EMPLOYMENT
IN TAIWAN, 1960, 1970, 1975

Occupation	Percentage of Population		
	1960	1970	1975
Agriculture and fishing	56.14	45.30	36.60
Manufacturing and mining	11.28	11.70	23.50
Commerce	8.91	8.50	8.80
Transportation	2.96	3.50	4.70
Services	16.70	26.70	26.30

From Table I one can see the population in agriculture has decreased from 56.14 percent in 1960 to 36.60 percent in 1975. Taiwan has limited farmland for agriculture (13, p. 187), and it is estimated that 50,000 persons have to leave the farm each year (14, p. 165). The population engages in industry, manufacturing in particular, has increased from 11.70 percent in 1960 and 1970 to 23.50 percent in 1975. At the same time, the population in services has increased from 16.70 percent to 26.70 percent in 1970 and to 26.30 percent in 1975.

As a whole, the decrease in the population in agriculture has had important impacts on the family. As the population in agriculture has decreased ten percent in the past five years and the population in manufacturing has increased ten percent in the same period, it is evident that the surplus population in agriculture have left the farm and looked for employment in manufacturing and other categories of occupations. In the future, these youths will establish their families in the place of their work in the cities and will gradually deviate from the traditional family pattern. That happened in the mainland in the Republican Period (35, p. 11).

The development in industrialization will continue in Nationalist China in the future as the Nationalist Government has adopted a Six-Year Economic Development Plan, beginning in 1976 and ending in 1981 (14, p. 164). In this plan, "the accelerated progress of industrialization has led to a steady increase in the variety and quantity of industrial products. Employment and labor productivity in the manufacturing sector also have been rising rapidly." (14, p. 178) The fast expansion of Taiwan's industry has resulted from the rapid increase of exports of light industrial products (14, p. 178).

Urbanization in Nationalist China

Due to the limited farmland for agriculture and the rapid development of industrialization, Nationalist China has about three-fifths of the population living in cities and towns and the remainder in rural areas (12, p. 103). Besides, about one-fourth of her population lived in five of the biggest cities in 1976, namely, Taipei with a population of 2,043,318, Kaohsiung 998,919, Keelung 341,383, Taichung 546,838, and Tainan 523,568 (14, pp. 131-132).

It is in the urban areas where new ideas are introduced. With the concentration of educational institutions, the mass media such as newspapers, motion pictures and television, and associations of various kinds, people are exposed to new ideas. Such a process of change and socialization happened in the mainland in the Republican Period before (35, p. 16). Therefore, when the youths leave the rural country to look for employment in the cities, they will no longer be subjected to the dominance of their parents and the traditional family patterns in the country.

The Continuous Influence of the Western Culture

The influence of the western culture on the family in Taiwan cannot be determined as the influence of the traditional Confucian ethical teachings have been strong in Taiwan (14, pp. 338-339). However, the influences of the western family structure have been quite significant on the family of orientation among university students (22, pp. 117-134).

A significant and critical factor which could have decisive impacts on the influence and acceptance of the western culture on Nationalist China, especially the American culture, is the prospect of the normalization of diplomatic relations between the U.S.A. and Communist China. The Nationalist Government has been very sensitive and cautious on any diplomatic move between the U.S.A. and Communist China (2, 5-8). As the U.S.A. is the only major world power today which still has formal diplomatic relations with Nationalist China and recognizes the legal status of Nationalist China as the official representative of China, the Nationalist Government would feel a severe diplomatic setback and betrayal of an ally if the U.S.A. will recognize Communist China, replacing Nationalist China, as the official representative of China. If the normalization of diplomatic relations between the U.S.A. and Communist China becomes a reality, the relationships between the U.S.A. and Nationalist China would be severely curtailed. It is predictable that Nationalist China would no longer view and accept the American culture with a favorable and welcoming attitude. As a consequence, the influence of the western culture on the family in Taiwan might be lessened at the same time.

Needed to be mentioned at the same time is the relationship between education and the family. In the first five months in 1977, there has been evidence that the parents of the students studying abroad, in the U.S.A. in particular, have shown great concern for the future careers of their children who have found it very difficult to secure employment and permanent residence visas to stay in foreign countries, in the U.S.A. in particular (33, p. 38). Several meetings of governments at the local levels were sponsored, by the Nationalist Government, in several cities and districts of Taiwan to contact the parents of the students studying abroad. In those meetings, the parents urged the Nationalist Government to provide employment for their children in Taiwan as those students would return to Taiwan after the completion of their education (3, 4, 6). The Nationalist Government promised to provide more employment for the returning students as the economy and industry in Taiwan has been expanding rapidly in the past five years since the early 1970's (9).

In looking toward the future of the family in Nationalist China, it is quite possible to believe that with the progress of industrialization and urbanization and the continuous influence of the western culture, if these are not disrupted by political reasons, the family in Nationalist China will gradually deviate further from the traditional family structure based on the Confucian ethics; and at the same time it will gradually move towards the ideal structure described in the Civil Code of 1930, namely, the family law of Nationalist China or the law of kinship relations.

The Future Trends of the Family in Communist China

The future trends of the family in Communist China are more difficult to predict as they will depend on the policy of the Communist leadership and the priorities of the Communist Government. The year 1976 was a very crucial transitional period for the Communists as their two most important leaders, the former Chairman Mao Tse-Tung and Premier Chou En-Lai passed away. The succession to the Party leadership also went through a stormy period as the four top-ranking radical leaders attempted to set up a second armed force and usurp the leadership of the national government. However, the four radical leaders were arrested by Hua, Kuo-Feng, the Party successor appointed by Mao Tse-Tung as the new Chairman of the Central Committee of the Communist Party.

The Policy of the Communist Leadership

The Communist leadership headed by Hua, Kuo-Feng will follow closely the policy established by Mao Tse-Tung. It can be seen in Hua's important speech (19, pp. 31-44), and Mao's political directive "On the Ten Major Relationships" was once again used as a guideline to direct the Party and the nation (23, pp. 10-25). Besides, Volume V of Selected Works of Mao Tse-Tung was published and distributed to the whole nation in April 1977 (28, pp. 5-6, 12-37). All these incidences indicate that the new Communist leadership will follow closely the policies of the former leadership headed by Mao Tse-Tung. Thus, the policy towards the family will not be changed. At least there are no indications to the contrary.

For example, youths from the city are still being sent to the countryside to work as peasants as they were in the 1960's in the past ten years and they have had problems of adjustments and adaptations to the new environment (1, pp. 75-108). Because many of them were not able to enter the university, correspondence courses were offered to them from the universities in the city (32, pp. 11-30).

In agriculture the goals accepted in 1962 (17, p. 12) and in 1975 (16, p. 6) were again repeated in the Agriculture Conference in December 1976 (17, pp. 11-15). The goals and principles in industry in 1977 (36, pp. 13-16, 18-23) were the same as those accepted in the 1960's (15, pp. 58-72; 29, p. 19).

The Priorities of the Communist Government

As the transition of the Party leadership went through a stormy period in 1976, there are several priorities the Communists want to achieve for the years to come. Those priorities will be grouped and examined as follows:

1. To deepen the great mass movement to expose and criticize the "Gang of Four" and strengthen Party building. As the four top-ranking radical leaders, the so-called anti-Party "gang of four," namely Wang Hung-Wen, Chang Chun-Chiao, Chiang Ching and Yao Wen-Yuan, dominated the Party bureaucracy for the past ten years since the Cultural Revolution (25, pp. 5-10; 18, pp. 9-12; 26, pp. 10-12). As a result, it has brought enormous difficulties to the leadership of the Party and the Government (19, p. 33). Thus, the new leadership has to eliminate the followers of those four radical leaders in the Party and the government of all levels (19, p. 38).

Of course, the next important step is to strengthen Party leadership after the disruptions in the past few years. Thus, the Central Committee of the Communist Party is going to launch a movement of Party consolidation and rectification throughout the Party and to strengthen the Party's unified leadership and centralism (19, pp. 39-41). At the same time, Hua Kuo-Feng will have to prove himself to the nation as the capable successor of the Chairman of the Central Committee of the Communist Party of China since he has been new to the Party leadership in Peking (21, pp. 5-11; 27, pp. 9-12; 20, pp. 15-27).

2. To push the national economy forward. Perhaps due to the power

struggle for the leadership in the Party, the national economy has not been advanced as expected (16, pp. 6-11; 10, pp. 6-9; 31, pp. 17-20, 32). Therefore, two national conferences were held in Peking, one for agriculture in December 1976 and the other for industry in April 1977. In agriculture, the goals are to step up the pace of farm mechanization, raise the high level of scientific farming and make the communes bigger in scale (24, pp. 5-17; 17, pp. 11-15). In industry, the goal is to achieve the comprehensive modernization of agriculture, industry, national defense, science and technology and to persevere in taking China's own road of industrial development (29, pp. 15-17; 30, pp. 7-14, 3-5, 15-24).

The two top priorities in Communist China are political and economic in nature for the years to come and have not included the family reorganization. Because of his newly established leadership in the Communist Government, Hua Kuo-Feng, its new leader, will take years to establish his influence and control over the nation. Due to the urgent needs of the party unity and the economy, the Communists most likely will neglect for years to come to transform the family according to the Communist model.

However, for the long term trend, with the passing away of the older generations raised under the form of the traditional family and the continuous political indoctrinations by the Communists on the younger generations, it is possible to believe that the dominance of the age and sex hierarchy in the family will be weakened. The speed of change in the family will be faster in urban than rural areas.

Recommendations for Further Studies

The Age and Sex Hierarchy in the Chinese Family

1. In traditional China, on the age hierarchy, studies on the causes for the establishment of the patriarchal system and the status, roles and power of the patriarch would be interesting. So also would be studies to show how closely the ideal and the actual family structures coincided.

On the sex hierarchy, studies can be made on the historical development of the emphasis on the father-son relationship through different eras and dynasties. As the ideal structure of the "law of clan organization" was supported by the rulers in traditional China, it would be essential to examine to what extent the ideal and the actual structures of the sex hierarchy coincided throughout the history of China, namely, through different eras or dynasties.

On the family as the center of loyalty, studies on the impacts and influences of such a family structure on the personality of the individual members and interrelation with other social institutions in the traditional society would have considerable academic values.

On the cult of ancestor worship, studies on the impacts of ancestor worship on the personality of the family members and as a mechanism of social control would be rewarding.

141

On the encouragement of the large family, the power structure and the way of life and the interrelations in those families would be interesting studies. One possible resource would be the semi-fiction such as The Dream of the Red Chamber.

Although the traditional family began to disintegrate after the establishment of the Republic in 1912, there are still possible resources for further studies. The review of literature, including historical data, could be one; and the selected interviews with older generations who lived in the form of the traditional family would be the other. Besides, participant observations in the rural family in Taiwan and Hong Kong could observe the remnant of the traditional family because traditions in the rural areas have been slow to change.

2. In the Republican Period, the traditional age and sex hierarchies in the family were under criticism and attacks. It was a period of change and transition. There are considerable amounts of historical and sociological data available for research; and interviews with the older generations as that period had significant impacts on the social and cultural changes in modern China. The causes and impacts of the changes in that period would be rewarding studies as the changes in the Republican Period led to further changes in the recent period.

3. In Nationalist China, the changes in the age and sex hierarchies have been under the influence of the western ideas, such as freedom and equality. Researches on the age and sex hierarchies on the non-intellectual classes are needed as most of the sociological research on the family have used university students as samples. Striking conflicts between the older and the younger generations are essential as well as studies of the status and roles of the females in the family in different social classes. Taiwan is opened for researchers to conduct their studies and many facilities are available, such as the universities and libraries.

4. In Communist China, the changes in the age and sex hierarchies have been generated by the Communist Government; and it is therefore essential to observe the impacts and influences of such changes in the age and sex hierarchies in the family. It would be rewarding to examine the closeness of the ideal and the actual structures. When the Communists tried to generate certain changes, it would be essential to examine how the people respond to such changes demanded by the Communists.

Since survey research is not allowed to be conducted in Communist China by outsiders, one possible resource is to interview the refugees who had left Communist China or visitors who were allowed to visit the country. While eighty percent of the nation's population live in the rural areas, studies on the urban population in the age and sex hierarchies have been neglected. It is believed that the urban population is more liberal than the rural one. Studies on the social changes in the urban areas would be rewarding because many of the important political and social activities are concentrated in urban areas.

Education and the Family in China

a) In traditional China, it would be interesting to have further studies on the affinity between education and the family and how the

142

family's influence could have assisted the motivation and success of the candidates for the civil service examinations and how education had influenced the role performance of the patriarch. There is plenty of literature for further studies on the education in traditional China, especially the educational thought of the Confucian school. The study on the affinity between education and the family could be found from historical records, such as the civil service examinations, the family background of the prominent officials, etc.

b) In the Republican Period, the traditional educational thought of the Confucian school was under attack and challenge and later was replaced by the Three Principles of the People. Further studies can be made on the reactions and adjustments of the family on the change of the educational policy of the nation to a new era, and later how the family had accepted the new educational policy. There are plenty of materials available for further studies, including literature and selected interviews with the older generations.

c) In Nationalist China, further studies are needed on the influences and impacts of the family's socialization on the students for the latter to use further studies abroad as a means for the purpose to stay permanently in the foreign countries. Besides, studies are needed to find out the other reasons for the students to leave the country other than those reasons given and accused by the official organs on the students and their families, such as the economic, social and political environments in Taiwan.

Studies can be made by selected interviews with professionals and students from Taiwan who are in the U.S.A. as permanent residents. Selected interviews can be made with those students who have returned to Taiwan reluctantly or willingly; and the opinions and plans and the family reactions of their return to Taiwan.

d) In Communist China, studies are needed on the final destiny of those intellectuals from the bourgeois family background who had been used and later replaced by the Communists, especially in the Cultural Revolution. How were those bourgeois intellectuals torn apart between their loyalty to the Communists and their bourgeois family, if they were?

Studies are also needed on the new admission policy after the Cultural Revolution and the sending of the youths from the city to the countryside. After the new admission policy was put into practice, what has been the academic standing and achievement of those students who were admitted into the university mainly on the basis of their family background and their political and work performance? What would be the status and rewards of the new college graduates? Will they and their families form an elite stratum? Is the new admission policy actually carried out as it is published?

Millions of youths were sent from the city to the countryside to live and work with the peasants. It would be rewarding to study their reactions concerning their own future career, their reactions towards the Communist Party and their links with their families.

As only a limited number of westerners can visit Communist China, reports from those visitors would be useful to obtain firsthand knowl-

edge. However, Chinese nationals who had established their residence
in Hong Kong could enter the China Mainland in large numbers. Therefore, selected interviews with those Chinese visitors and the refugees
who had left Communist China in the past few years can provide useful
and genuine information and data for further studies.

BIBLIOGRAPHY--CHAPTER XI

1. Bernstein, Thomas P., "Urban Youths in the Countryside: Problems of Adaptation and Remedies," China Quarterly, London, March 1977, pp. 75-108.

2. Taipei, Central Daily News, April 15, 1977.

3. _____, _____ _____ ____, April 23, 1977.

4. _____, _____ _____ ____, April 25, 1977.

5. _____, _____ _____ ____, April 28, 1977.

6. _____, _____ _____ ____, April 29, 1977.

7. _____, _____ _____ ____, April 30, 1977.

8. _____, _____ _____ ____, May 16, 1977.

9. _____, _____ _____ ____, May 22, 1977.

10. Chi, Wei, "How the 'Gang of Four' Opposed Socialist Modernization," Peking Review, March 11, 1977, 6-9.

11. China Yearbook, 1961-62. Taipei, China Publishing Co., 1962.

12. China Yearbook, 1971-72. Taipei, China Publishing Co., 1972.

13. China Yearbook, 1975. Taipei, China Publishing Co., 1975.

14. China Yearbook, 1976. Taipei, China Publishing Co., 1976.

15. "The Most Beautiful, The Most Up-To-Date Picture," Chinese Sociology and Anthropology, New York, Fall 1976, 58-72.

16. Chou, Chin, "A Year of Advance Amid Storms," at the Second National Learn-From-Tachai Conference, Peking Review, February 11, 1977, 6-10.

17. Chou, Chin, "Mechanization: Fundamental Way Out for Agriculture," at the Second National Learn-From-Tachai Conference, Peking Review, February 25, 1977, 11-15.

18. Hsieh, Cheng, "Ferreting Out 'the Bourgeoisie in the Army' - Another 'Gang of Four' Scheme," Peking Review, March 4, 1977, 9-12.

19. Hua, Kuo-Feng, "Speech at the Second National Conference on Learning From Tachai in Agriculture," Peking Review, January 1, 1977, pp. 38-41.

20. Hua, Kuo-Feng, "Continue the Revolution Under the Dictatorship of the Proletariat - A Study of Volume V of the 'Selected Works of Mao Tse-Tung'" Peking Review, May 6, 1977, 15-27.

21. Jen, Hua, "Comrade Hua Kuo-Feng in Hunan," Peking Review, February

25, 1977, 5-11.

22. Lung, Kwan-Hai and Shiao-Chun Chang, "A Study of the Chinese Family Organization," Journal of Sociology, No. 3, April 1967, National Taiwan University, 117-134.

23. Mao, Tse-Tung, "On the Ten Major Relationships," Peking Review, January 1, 1977, 10-25.

24. "Comrade Chen Yung-Kuei's Reports - at the Second National Conference on Learning from Tachai in Agriculture," Peking Review, January 7, 1977, 5-17.

25. "How the 'Gang of Four' Used Shanghai as a Base to Usurp Party and State Party," Peking Review, February 4, 1977, 5-10.

26. "Failure of 'Gang of Four' Scheme to Set Up a 'Second Armed Force,'" Peking Review, March 25, 1977, 10-12.

27. "Comrade Hua Kuo-Feng in the Years of War," Peking Review, April 8, 1977, 9-12.

28. "Volume V of 'Selected Works of Mao Tse-Tung,' Published and Distributed," Peking Review, April 22, 1977, 5-6, 12-37.

29. "National Conference on Learning from Taching in Industry Opens," Peking Review, April 29, 1977, 3-6, 15-24.

30. "Chairman Hua Kuo-Feng's Speech - at the National Conference on Learning from Taching in Industry," Peking Review, May 20, 1977, 7-14, 15-24.

31. "Taching Fights the 'Four Pests,'" Peking Review, June 10, 1977, 17-20, 32.

32. The Shanghai Municipal Bureau of Education, "Correspondence Universities Have Made Great Achievement," Chinese Education, New York, Winter 1976-77, 11-30.

33. U. S. Department of Justice, Immigration and Naturalization Service, 1975 Annual Report: Immigration and Naturalization Service, Washington, D.C. 1975.

34. Wolf, Margery, Women and the Family in Rural Taiwan, Stanford, Stanford University Press, 1972.

35. Yang, Ch'ing-K'un, Chinese Communist Society: The Family and the Village, Cambridge, Massachusetts Institute of Technology Press, 1972. 5th ed. copyright 1959.

CHAPTER 12

DEVELOPMENT SINCE 1977

Toward the end of 1977, considerable changes were made on the college enrollment system. On November 11, 1977, the "New College Enrollment System" was published in Peking Review as follows:

Under the new system, all young workers, peasants (including educated young people who have settled in the country-side), demobilized armymen, Party and government functionaries and this year's senior middle school graduates can voluntarily apply and take college entrance examinations, provided they have given a good account of themselves politically, have a schooling equivalent to that of senior middle school and are physically fit. This also applies to senior middle school students who are up to the educational level of a graduate (p. 16).

Such a new procedure of application for college enrollment has eliminated many of the controls and limitations on the students in previous years as they candidates themselves can apply directly now for the examination. Besides, the educational level of the candidates is also emphasized.

As opposed to previous years when almost all the senior middle school graduates were sent to labor at least for two years in the country-side or in factories, about 20 to 30 percent of college students will be enrolled from among senior middle school graduates of the current year (p. 16). Of course, such a direct recruitment will be beneficial as the high school graduates need not lay down their studies for two years.

Also, the emphasis of recruitment has been shifted from political to intellectual emphasis, as

in order to let as many talents young people as possible acquire higher education, attention is also paid to enrolling outstanding barefoot doctors, primary school teachers and young people actively engaged in agro-science and techniques from the rural areas as well as students of minority nationalities and a certain number of young people of Taiwan Province origin and young Chinese from Hong Kong, Macao and abroad.
    An all-round appraisal will be made of the applicants morally, intellectually and physically. Entrance examinations will be restored and admittance based on their results (p. 17).

However, the family background of the candidates is also emphasized, as "a series of effective measures have been taken to increase annually among workers and peasants and their children, thus ensuring in a fairly short time that they form the majority in college." (p. 17).

Besides, the wage has been raised from many workers since October 1977 as recorded in Peking Review (December 2, 1977, pp. 3, 27). The raise affects about 46 percent of the total number of workers and staff. Included are industrial workers, workers and staff in the commercial and service trades, teachers, scientific and technical workers, medical personnel, literary and art workers and government functionaries (p. 3).

Also economic developments have been strongly emphasized since 1977 (Peking Review, December 2, 1977, pp. 4-8; January 6, 1978, pp. 7, 11).

APPENDIX

THE MARRIAGE LAW OF THE PEOPLE'S REPUBLIC OF CHINA

CHAPTER I

GENERAL PRINCIPLES

ARTICLE 1

The feudal marriage system based on arbitrary and compulsory arrangements and the supremacy of man over woman, and in disregard of the interests of the children, is abolished.

The New-Democratic marriage system, which is based on the free choice of partners, on monogamy, on equal rights for both sexes, and on the protection of the lawful interests of women and children, is put into effect.

ARTICLE 2

Bigamy, concubinage, child betrothal, interference in the re-marriage of widows, and the exaction of money or gifts in connection with marriages, are prohibited.

CHAPTER II

THE MARRIAGE CONTRACT

ARTICLE 3

Marriage is based upon the complete willingness of the two parties. Neither party shall use compulsion and no third party is allowed to interfere.

ARTICLE 4

A marriage can be contracted only after the man has reached 20 years of age and the woman 18 years of age.

ARTICLE 5

No man or woman is allowed to marry in any of the following instances:

a) Where the man and woman are lineal relatives by blood or where the man and woman are brother and sister born of the same parents or where the man and woman are half-brother and half-sister. The question of prohibiting marriage between collateral relatives by blood (up to the fifth degree of relationship) is determined by custom.

b) Where one party, because of certain physical defects, is sexually impotent.

c) Where one party is suffering from venereal disease, mental disorder, leprosy or any other disease which is regarded by medical science as rendering a person unfit for marriage.

ARTICLE 6

In order to contract a marriage, both the man and the woman should register in person with the people's government of the district or township in which they reside. If the proposed marriage is found to be in conformity with the provisions of this Law, the local people's government should, without delay, issue marriage certificates.

If the proposed marriage is not found to be in conformity with the provisions of this Law, registration should not be granted.

CHAPTER III

RIGHTS AND DUTIES OF HUSBAND AND WIFE

ARTICLE 7

Husband and wife are companions living together and enjoy equal status in the home.

ARTICLE 8

Husband and wife are in duty bound to love, respect, assist and look after each other, to live in harmony, to engage in productive work, to care for their children and to strive jointly for the welfare of the family and for the building up of the new society.

ARTICLE 9

Both husband and wife have the right to free choice of occupation and free participation in work or in social activities.

ARTICLE 10

Husband and wife have equal rights in the possession and management of family property.

ARTICLE 11

Husband and wife have the right to use his or her own family name.

ARTICLE 12

Husband and wife have the right to inherit each other's property.

CHAPTER IV

RELATIONS BETWEEN PARENTS AND CHILDREN

ARTICLE 13

Parents have the duty to rear and to educate their children; the children have the duty to support and to assist their parents. Neither the parents nor the children shall maltreat or desert one another.

The foregoing provision also applies to foster-parents and foster-children.

Infanticide by drowning and similar criminal acts are strictly prohibited.

ARTICLE 14

Parents and children have the right to inherit one another's property.

ARTICLE 15

Children born out of wedlock enjoy the same rights as children born in lawful wedlock. No person is allowed to harm them or discriminate against them.

Where the paternity of a child born out of wedlock is legally established by the mother of the child or by other witnesses or material evidence, the identified father must bear the whole or part of the cost of maintenance and education of the child until the age of 18.

With the consent of the mother, the natural father may have custody of the child.

With regard to the maintenance of a child born out of wedlock, if its mother marries, the provisions of Article 22 apply.

ARTICLE 16

Niether husband nor wife may maltreat or discriminate against children born of a previous marriage by either party and in that party's custody.

CHAPTER V

DIVORCE

ARTICLE 17

Divorce is granted when husband and wife both desire it. In the event of either the husband or the wife alone insisting upon divorce, it may be granted only when mediation by the district people's government and the judicial organ has failed to bring about a reconciliation.

In cases where divorce is desired by both husband and wife, both parties should register with the district people's government in order to obtain divorce certificates. The district people's government, after establishing that divorce is desired by both parties and that appropriate measures have been taken for the care of children and property, should issue the divorce certificates without delay.

When one party insists on divorce, the district people's government may try to effect a reconciliation. If such mediation fails, it should, without delay, refer the case to the county or municipal people's court for decision. The district people's government should not attempt to prevent or to obstruct either party from appealing to the county or municipal people's court. In dealing with a divorce case, the county or municipal people's court should, in the first instance, try to bring about a reconciliation between the parties. In case such mediation fails, the court should render a decision without delay.

After divorce, if both husband and wife desire the resumption of marriage relations, they should apply to the district people's government for a registration of re-marriage. The district people's government should accept such a registration and issue certificates of re-marriage.

ARTICLE 18

The husband is not allowed to apply for a divorce when his wife is pregnant, and may apply for divorce only one year after the birth of the child. In the case of a woman applying for divorce, this restriction does not apply.

ARTICLE 19

In the case of a member of the revolutionary army on active service who maintains correspondence with his or her family, that army member's consent must be obtained before his or her spouse can apply for divorce.

Divorce may be granted to the spouse of a member of the revolutionary army who does not correspond with his or her family for a period of two years subsequent to the date of the promulgation of this Law. Divorce may also be granted to the spouse of a member of the revolutionary army, who had not maintained correspondence with his or her family for over two years prior to the promulgation of this Law, and who fails to correspond with his or her family for a further period of one year subsequent to the promulgation of the present law.

CHAPTER VI

MAINTENANCE AND EDUCATION OF CHILDREN AFTER DIVORCE

ARTICLE 20

The blood ties between parents and children are not ended by the divorce of the parents. No matter whether the father or the mother has the custody of the children, they remain the children of both parties.

After divorce, both parents continue to have the duty to support and educate their children.

After divorce, the guiding principle is to allow the mother to have the custody of a breast-fed infant. After the weaning of the child, if a dispute arises between the two parties over the guardianship and an agreement cannot be reached, the people's court should render a decision in accordance with the interests of the child.

ARTICLE 21

If, after divorce, the mother is given custody of a child, the father is responsible for the whole or part of the necessary cost of the maintenance and education of the child. Both parties should reach an agreement regarding the amount and the duration of such maintenance and education. Lacking such an agreement, the people's court should render a decision.

Payment may be made in cash, in kind or by tilling land allocated to the child.

An agreement reached between parents or a decision rendered by the people's court in connection with the maintenance and education of a child does not obstruct the child from requesting either parent to increase the amount decided upon by agreement or by judicial decision.

ARTICLE 22

In the case where a divorced woman re-marries and her husband is willing to pay the whole or part of the cost of maintaining and educating the child or children by her former husband, the father of the child or children is entitled to have such cost of maintenance and education reduced or to be exempted from bearing such cost in accordance with the circumstances.

CHAPTER VII

PROPERTY AND MAINTENANCE AFTER DIVORCE

ARTICLE 23

In case of divorce, the wife retains such property as belonged to her prior to her marriage. The disposal of other family property is subject to agreement between the two parties. In cases where agreement cannot be reached, the people's court should render a decision after taking into consideration the actual state of the family property, the interests of the wife and the child or children, and the principle of benefiting the development of production.

In cases where the property allocated to the wife and her child or children is sufficient for the maintenance and education of the child or children, the husband may be exempted from bearing further maintenance and education costs.

ARTICLE 24

In case of divorce, debts incurred jointly by husband and wife during the period of their married life should be paid out of the property jointly acquired by them during this period. In cases where no such property has been acquired or in cases where such property is insufficient to pay off such debts, the husband is held responsible for paying them. Debts incurred separately by the husband or wife should be paid off by the party responsible.

ARTICLE 25

After divorce, if one party has not re-married and has maintenance difficulties, the other party should render assistance. Both parties should work out an agreement with regard to the method and duration of such assistance; in case an agreement cannot be reached, the people's court should render a decision.

CHAPTER VIII

BY-LAWS

ARTICLE 26

Persons violating this Law will be punished in accordance with law. In cases where interference with the freedom of marriage has caused death or injury to one or both parties, persons guilty of such interference will bear responsibility for the crime before the law.

ARTICLE 27

This Law comes into force from the date of its promulgation.

In regions inhabited by minority nationalities in compact communities, the people's government (or the Military and Administrative Committee) of the Greater Administrative Area or the provincial people's government may enact certain modifications or supplementary articles in conformity with the actual conditions prevailing among minority nationalities in regard to marriage. But such measures must be submitted to the Government Administration Council for ratification before enforcement.

First Edition   1950
Third Edition   1973
Second Printing   1975

Foreign Languages Press, Peking
Printed in the People's Republic of China